The Third World
Problems and Perspectives

The Third World
Problems and Perspectives

Edited by
Alan B. Mountjoy

*Published
in association with*
The Geographical Magazine

MACMILLAN

First published 1978
Reprinted 1980 (twice), 1981, 1983, 1986

Published by
MACMILLAN EDUCATION LTD
Houndmills, Basingstoke, Hampshire RG21 2XS
and London
Companies and representatives
throughout the world

Printed in Hong Kong

British Library Cataloguing in Publication Data

The Third World: problems and perspectives.
  1. Underdeveloped areas – Social conditions
  – Addresses, essays, lectures
  I. Mountjoy, Alan Bertram II. 'Geographical
  Magazine'
  309.2'3'91724   HN980

  ISBN 0–333–24814–7
  ISBN 0–333–24815–5 Pbk

Contents

5

6 *Contents*

List of Maps and Diagrams

List of Plates

1 Village school in Nepal
2 Degree ceremony at an African university
3 Malnutrition in Indonesia
4 Wind-driven irrigation pump, Ethiopia
5 A New Guinea family
6 An Indian family planning clinic
7 Labour-intensive public work in Egypt
8 Camel-owning nomads of North Kordofan
9 Hand winnowing of rice, Pakistan
10 Buffalo cart, Pakistan
11 Demonstration of rice and fertiliser tests, Java
12 Coconut palm nursery, Ghana
13 An agrarian reform co-operative, Egypt
14 Intermediate technology in Sri Lanka
15 Cassava grinder, Nigeria
16 Transport on a laterite road, Upper Volta
17 Bicycle versatility, Mali
18 Brick making, Brazil
19 A labour-intensive industry, Sudan
20 The Volta Redonda iron and steel works, Brazil
21 Engineering training, Cairo
22 'Cardboard Town', Khartoum
23 Shanty town industries, Freetown
24 Shanty squalor, Bangkok
25 Squatter rehousing, Singapore

List of Tables

The cover illustration, depicting children begging for food in India, is reproduced by permission of *The Geographical Magazine* and the John Topham Picture Library, Edenbridge, Kent.

Preface

This book was first mooted some time ago at a conference on Development held at a university in southern England. Nearly all those present were economists, keen to discuss theories and models of development which, to the few geographers present, seemed far removed from the realities of the African bush or the padi lands of South-east Asia. It was this need for reality, to get one's feet on the ground in the understanding of Third World problems, that led to discussion and eventually to the series of articles in *The Geographical Magazine* that are now incorporated in this volume.

The aim of this book is modest: to present factually a wide spectrum of the ills and problems of the Third World and to make some assessment of the state of developing countries today after a quarter of a century of efforts at economic development. The complexity of interrelationships is simplified by a division of the material into 14 parts: this is a convenient method of analysis and at the same time offers a series of topics for further discussion. A primary object of the authors has been to give a basis for such discussion and thus to facilitate understanding of the problems of poverty, and its removal, that affect between two and three thousand million people and in which we, in our more fortunate conditions, are becoming increasingly involved.

All the authors are specialists in the fields on which they write and the articles have been expanded and updated since they first appeared in *The Geographical Magazine*. Lists of books and articles for further reading and an index have also been provided. Thanks are due to Mr Derek Weber, editor of *The Geographical Magazine* for his patient help and enthusiasm for the series, and to the photographic and cartographic staff of the Department of Geography, Bedford College (University of London), who have prepared the maps and diagrams.

Bedford College, London   A.B.M.
March 1978

1
The Third World in Perspective

Alan B. Mountjoy

What do we mean by the Third World? This title has become a convenient omnibus term for the world's underdeveloped countries. It came into vogue during the 1960s and embraces a third element in the world power structure. Our world is dominated by the 'free world' of the Atlantic bloc and the centrally organised European communist bloc. They comprise the technologically advanced nations but hold only 40 per cent of the world land surface and a minority 30 per cent of the world's population. There remains a vast community of independent nations, most recently emerged from the colonial era, to be found mainly in the lower latitudes: they comprise the Third World. In this group are the poorest nations in the world, technologically backward but capable of great advances and possessing in their territories a great wealth of mineral, vegetable and energy resources. In the strict sense they are not a homogenous bloc separate from the two advanced power groups, for in their poverty they seek patronage and help, and lean to one group or the other.

A succession of descriptive names has been applied to the countries of the Third World – backward nations, undeveloped, under-developed, then developing (a more dynamic term); now 'Less-Developed Countries' (LDCs) is in vogue. All these countries are poor: they have been left behind by the accelerating economic progress of the nations of mainly European stock in the temperate climatic belts. Whichever data are used to define the less-developed countries – Gross National Product (GNP) per head, the net *per capita* income, amount of energy per head of population, the literacy rate – a similar pattern emerges and the startling imbalance in the distribution of the world's wealth is revealed. The range between the richest and poorest nations is dreadfully wide; the income per head in the United Kingdom, which

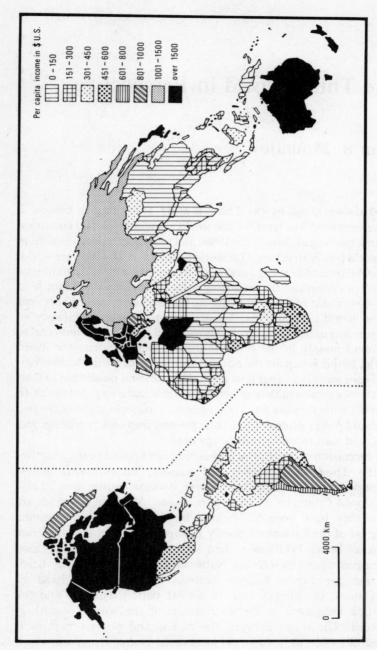

Figure 1 World *per capita* net incomes in US $ (c. 1970)

Per capita income in $ U.S.

	0 – 150
	151 – 300
	301 – 450
	451 – 600
	601 – 800
	801 – 1000
	1001 – 1500
	over 1500

0   4000 km

is now well down the list of 'rich nations', is fifteen to twenty times that of the world's poorest countries. There the notional income per head may be as low as £20 a year – a figure far below what British trades unions seek as the nation's minimum wage per week. It is a deplorable fact that more than half the world's population has a *per capita* income of less than £40 per annum. Such poverty is utter and absolute and is endured today by hundreds of millions of human beings. With this poverty goes hunger and undernourishment. The current United Nations estimate is that up to 500 million people are now suffering from malnutrition. This is almost one-fifth of the total population of the Third World, but in many developing countries from one-quarter to one-third suffer from protein–calorie malnutrition.

If an arbitrary upper limit of $600 annual *per capita* income is set, the Third World embraces about 100 nations. It comprises 60 per cent of the earth's surface and is the home of about 70 per cent of the human race, some 2800 million people. By A.D. 2000 the population of the Third World could be as many as 5000 million. Their spread on the map should remind us of the diversity among less-developed countries of climate, terrain, geographical position, cultures, traditions, institutions and demographic situations. Too often homogeneity is assumed and LDCs are lumped together as being alike in order to satisfy this or that theory of economic development; each less-developed state has its own personality and its own particular problems.

Characteristics of Less-Developed Countries

Nevertheless less-developed countries do have many common characteristics in addition to their poverty. Their economies show a high proportion of subsistence agriculture with a very limited application of technology: manufacturing industry is minimal. Usually there is considerable reliance upon the export of one or two cash crops like coffee, cocoa, cotton, or rubber to the developed world. This puts economies at the mercy of fluctuating world prices and terms of trade. Certain common population characteristics are also evident. Expectation of life at birth in these countries is not very high: 39 years in Ethopia, and 41 in India as against 71 in the United Kingdom. Families tend to be large and thus there is a remarkably high

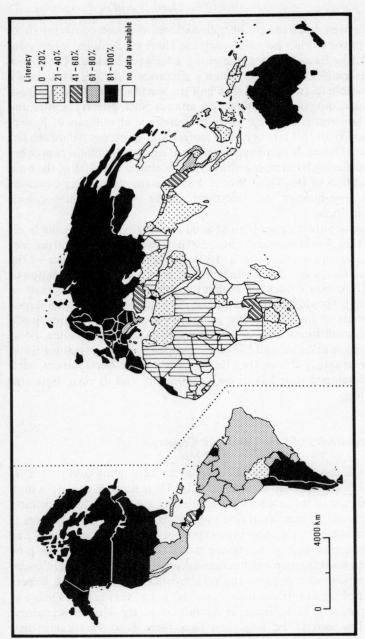

Figure 2 World levels of literacy (c. 1970)

proportion of young people in their populations, usually between 40 and 50 per cent, who consume goods and services but are not themselves productive. Education is a luxury long denied the mass of Third World peoples, consequently illiteracy rates are high. Women come off especially badly in this connection; for example the male illiteracy rate in Libya is 62.5 per cent, female 96 per cent; and in India, the male rate is 59 per cent, female rate 87 per cent.

In health also the developing world lags far behind the advanced world. Disease is a real factor in retarding the development of tropical areas. It is a dreadful fact that most of the population of the Third World is disease-ridden and undernourished. Nutrition diseases such as rickets, kwashiorkor, beri-beri and pellagra reduce the working capacity and condemn millions to early death. These diseases reduce resistance to such endemic scourges as malaria, yaws, typhoid, intestinal worm diseases, and smallpox. Ignorance, poor standards of hygiene and lack of medical facilities exacerbate this situation. A vicious circular pattern may be discerned: ill health = reduced working capacity = low productivity = poverty = undernourishment = ill health. It is the onslaught upon ill health supported by such bodies as the World Health Organization that is gradually bringing the effects of the 'medical revolution' to the Third World. The building and equipping of hospitals, the training of more doctors and nurses, the introduction of the new drugs and antibiotics, in most cases yet in a preliminary stage, is doing much to relieve suffering, to control disease and save lives.

Table 1 Number of Inhabitants per Physician

Afghanistan	31000	Mali	40000
Brazil	3600	Niger Republic	66000
Indonesia	19000	USA	700
	UK	830	

One of the most publicised effects of this medical revolution is its impact on the demographic pattern. Death rates are being reduced, especially infant mortality rates. The children whose lives are saved go on to live out a full lifespan. This is bringing about the 'juvenility' of these populations and as time passes enlarges the reproductive age group. In general, there has been no fall in birth rates matching the fall in the death rates and populations in the developing world are tending to grow at an ever-faster rate. Expanding population has both social and economic repercussions. People underemployed on the land increasingly are moving to the cities. There the high hopes of a better quality of life are dashed in the crowded shanty towns that are mushrooming around these cities and in the wearisome efforts to seek work and eke out an existence in an alien, unfriendly environment.

The rapid increase in the populations of many less-developed countries has helped to perpetuate poverty and malnutrition, for economic advances have become absorbed in supporting a larger number at subsistence level. The introduction of population policies to stabilise or even reduce populations are hard to apply among mainly uneducated, illiterate populations, and meet opposition not only from individuals but sometimes even at national level. The increasing numbers of children makes the provision and cost of schooling more difficult at a time when the spread of education is an indispensable foundation for emergence to a modern society.

International Concern

The concerted movement of the richer countries of the world to help their poorer neighbours has continued for more than two decades. It has grown with the increase of the world knowledge of underdevelopment and much of this emanated from the war years. During the Second World War hundreds of thousands of servicemen from the richer countries saw for themselves the poverty and backwardness of many alien lands. This helped to strip the blinkers from the eyes of people in the richer countries and they began to discover and understand for the first time the great gulf between themselves and their less fortunate fellow humans. Bodies such as the United Nations, the Food and Agricultural Organization and the World Health Organization, have assiduously collected and published facts and figures and given more precision to our knowledge of world underdevelopment and world poverty.

The poor also have become aware of their poverty and of the better life enjoyed by those who live in the developed countries. They have become less reconciled with their lot and have begun to press for change and improvement. The great period of decolonisation turned the attention of the colonial powers to the levels of well-being of the countries they were releasing, and this heightened the post-war sense of obligation which had grown following President Truman's Point Four. He publicly urged the American people to make the benefits of scientific advances and industrial progress available for the improvement of the world's poorer countries . . . ' For the first time in history, humanity possesses the knowledge and skill to relieve the suffering of these people'. In short, world sympathy and world conscience has been stirred and mounting programmes of technical and financial help and advice have been showered upon the Third World. Of course, more than uneasy feelings of conscience underlie policies of help for the poorer countries. To some extent the more advanced countries should benefit by a more efficient organisation of world productive capacity, from enlarged trade and from more stable conditions over the face of the globe. It is not all altruism. The growing awareness of worldwide inequality of economic development coincided with a growing confidence by economists in new theories of development and, indeed, of the emergence of development economics as an important part of their discipline.

The social, political and economic changes that converted Europe and North America from subsistence agricultural economies to the highly advanced industrial nations of today were spread over many decades: perhaps a century of trial and error, of discovery of new materials, of new technologies, of the creation of new organs of finance, of new commercial relationships, of changing social and political environments. It is recognised that the Third World cannot wait a century, nor is it necessary. The experiences, achievements and knowledge of Europe and North America are readily available. The know-how can be transferred, financial and technical aid is abundant. The development economists using these ingredients plan the desired social and economic metamorphism in a series of, usually, five- or seven-year plans. The need for careful planning to prevent waste of resources and to bring ordered and coordinated change is now beyond argument and from this the paramount role of the government is accepted. Yet despite over twenty years of endeavour and the investment of thousands of millions of pounds in the Third World no great breakthrough seems to have been achieved: some might say the reverse, for the gap between rich and poor continues to increase. The United Nations estimate of average national income per head in the developed world rose from $1360 in 1960 to about

$2700 in 1970. In the developing world the average income per head for 1960 was put at $130 rising only to $200 in 1970.

In an endeavour to focus attention upon this supreme world problem the United Nations designated the 1960s as the Development Decade. Member states coordinated their efforts in trade, financial and technical assistance to increase help to the developing countries and to speed their growth rate. One important outcome was the suggestion that the richer nations should endeavour to contribute capital and assistance at least at the level of one per cent of their combined national incomes. In fact, this level of aid was not attained and generally the results of the decade were disappointing; to some degree expectations had been pitched too high.

It is not the wisdom of aid that is now in doubt but its character. It has become more commercialised over the past two decades and it has become less and less satisfactory to the majority of receiving nations. The good-will and generous feelings of the early post-war period gradually changed, and too often aid has become an economic instrument supporting scarcely concealed political aims. Aid has been so directed by former colonial powers that it has helped preserve long-established economic, political and cultural ties. By tying the spending of much of the aid to the donor countries, it has helped the donors' industries and become a disguised subsidy for their exports. Even more serious has been the growing indebtedness of the developing countries: something like $250 000 million is owed and interest and amortisation payments in some developing countries take more than half the annual aid they are given. Third World countries are so heavily in debt that there is little likelihood of major repayment: they have come to look on aid as an instrument that prolongs and strengthens the richer nations' influence and power over them.

Now, in the late 1970s, we are nearing the end of the Second Development Decade. For this a target growth rate of 3.5 per cent of gross product per head is envisaged. Such an annual growth rate per head will double average income per head over twenty years. This target is calculated on the basis of an average annual growth rate of population in the less-developed countries of 2.5 per cent: this is actually less than the current average rate of increase and must cast doubts upon the realism of such calculations and targets.

Progress in Modernisation

Why has there been such disappointing progress after twenty years of international effort? High hopes in many poor countries have become blunted; the goodwill of the people of the richer nations has gone sour. The World Bank in its 1972 report said that 'it is probably true that the world's burden of poverty is increasing rather than declining.' Yet there has been some progress: over the last decade an annual growth rate of production and income of 3 per cent per head has been recorded for the developing world. Unfortunately much of this is attributable to marked advances in economic development by a small number of countries, such as Taiwan, South Korea, Malaysia, Brazil. Thus global figures hide a wide disparity of performance: for the majority of countries material advance has been small. Further, GNPs may be enlarged by the introduction of advanced industrial techniques but such operations are capital- rather than labour-intensive, they employ few people and thus either leave untouched or worsen the massive problems of unemployment and underemployment so prevalent in most of the developing world.

In the West there is a tendency to think of development in economic terms: the path towards the maximisation of goods and services per head. It does not follow that these values will be accepted by all the Third World countries, especially those with long cultural traditions of their own. Development implies more than economic growth: it means fundamental changes in society, in ways of life, in political and institutional patterns and the grasping of new concepts and new sets of values. The modernisation of economies encourages and in turn depends upon changes in social attitudes such as to the mobility of labour, the prestige of land or animal ownership, relations between landlord and tenant, the desirability of education, of birth control, the status of women, identity with the nation rather than the tribe. It should be clear that development is no simple, straightforward process of economics but strikes at the very roots of social and institutional patterns.

This is the heart of the matter and may explain why the enormous efforts and the dedicated enthusiasm of a massive international band of economists, agronomists, social anthropologists, engineers and others have seemingly made such moderate impact on this world problem. We must recognise the complexity of interlocking problems that have to be faced in this fight against poverty and backwardness by our first global mobilisation of energies and resources. The picture today is one of confusion and disappointment. In the following chapters we shall examine closely a varied range of aspects of this great problem, and by the analyses presented demonstrate inter-relationships, clarify the major issues, and make an assessment of Third World Progress after 25 years of effort.

2
Environmental Hazards in the Third World

Michael J. Eden

Throughout the developing world, diverse environmental limitations hinder man's attempts to exploit land resources. In many instances these limitations may be overcome by the application of modern technology, but even with effective organisation and finance success finally depends on the quality of the human resources involved. In developing countries such resources may be severely restricted.

Developing countries of low latitudes are characterised by a variety of physical conditions but one fundamental blessing is common to all. They enjoy a high availability of solar energy throughout the year, the resource upon which all biological productivity ultimately depends. It is essential to photosynthesis and plant growth, and the organic compounds thus created in turn sustain activity and growth in the animal kingdom.

Equally vital to biological growth is a supply of water. Geographically, the availability of water varies enormously through the developing world but in the humid tropics, at least, abundant water is available for biological growth for all or much of the year. This climatic régime is not without problems, however, for tropical rainfall is commonly intense as well as abundant. There is the danger of accelerated soil erosion where land is cleared for agriculture and the natural protection of vegetation removed. The hazard may be reduced, for example, by adopting cropping systems which minimise the extent to which the soil is bared, or on sloping land by the maintenance of terracing. Particularly in areas of greater relief, however, the land remains vulnerable. In the Andes of Colombia and Ecuador, the results of past negligence are clearly visible and large areas of land are badly eroded.

Soil limitations of other kinds are also encountered in the humid tropical zone. Prolonged weathering and leaching of the land surface, particularly in the older plainlands of Africa and South America, have given rise to soils of low fertility, even though they may support a luxuriant forest vegetation. Moreover, the nutrients which are present are rapidly leached if forest clearance occurs. These areas of latosolic and related soils are able to support unintensive shifting cultivation. But the development of more productive agriculture presents problems, and is likely to require costly fertiliser inputs before more intensive use of the land can be made. Elsewhere in the humid tropics, in parts of New Guinea or Indonesia for example, more fertile alluvial or volcanic soils may be encountered. Traditional cropping systems are often more intensive but natural fertility is likely to be inadequate as a basis for future land use.

In the sub-tropical zone, very different ecological conditions exist. Rainfall is often low and large variations occur in its availability from year to year; problems of water deficit, which may severely limit crop or livestock production, are paramount. Periodic dry farming may occur in these areas, and in places, particularly on alluvial lowlands adjoining large rivers, the problem has been overcome by irrigation agriculture. Irrigation has long been practised in the Nile and Indus valleys and further exploitation of externally derived river waters or untapped groundwaters offers considerable scope for its extension. Irrigation agriculture, however, can run into difficulties; in the lower Indus valley excessive application of irrigation water in the past has led to extensive waterlogging, soil salination, crop failure and land abandonment. Such problems have not always been avoided in more recent irrigation schemes. Elsewhere in the sub-tropical zone periodic droughts occur, and can produce acute problems for nomadic and cultivating peoples alike. Recent abnormally dry years in West African territories like Mali and Niger, for example, have created food shortages and severe human hardship. And these climatic conditions aggravate further the existing problem of the southward extension of the Sahara desert in this region.

Land development is influenced by various biological factors. An important one is the quality of crop varieties and livestock breeds utilised. Many in use today, although commonly tolerant of marginal environmental conditions or indifferent management, are not especially productive. Native cattle of the Indian village or Venezuelan ranch, hardy animals adapted to survive in highly competitive conditions or adverse environments, are not efficient meat or milk producers as are their European counterparts. Equally, many crop varieties adapted to poor soils or uncertain moisture regimes are not characterised by high yields per hectare.

There have been attempts to improve this situation in the developing world for many years. Cross breeding of high quality zebu cattle with native stock has made some impact on productivity in the savanna lands of Africa and South America; in places moves have been made to establish improved pastures for stock raising. More spectacular advances in the developing world are associated with basic food crops particularly the recent development of high yielding varieties of wheat, maize and rice. In countries like the Philippines and Cambodia, rice productivity has increased significantly in recent years, and many countries are experimenting with new crop varieties.

Pests, Diseases and Health

Pests and diseases pose an immense task for agriculturalists. As technological progress is achieved and increasing use made of new varieties, chemical fertilisers and irrigation waters, the damage imposed by pests and diseases on crops and stock becomes increasingly apparent and critical. 'Swollen shoot' disease in cocoa and 'rust' disease in coffee damage tropical cash crops and bring them to the attention of the European observer; but other hazards such as 'blast' disease in rice and stalk borers in maize are more destructive of local food production. Pests such as locusts destroying crops in the field and rats destroying them in store also require constant control. However, care is necessary here. For example, careless application of pesticides can be counterproductive by upsetting the natural faunal balance. One of the effects of this may be that previously minor insect populations increase in size, and attain the status of pests as their predators are destroyed. Crop losses will continue.

Livestock productivity is limited by disease. In tropical Africa, tsetse fly transmits the cattle disease trypanosomiasis and limits, in many cases prohibits, the keeping of cattle over large areas. Elsewhere, foot and mouth disease is particularly difficult to control under 'open range' conditions.

Environmental and biological factors severely limit land productivity. Limitations can often be overcome by modern technology

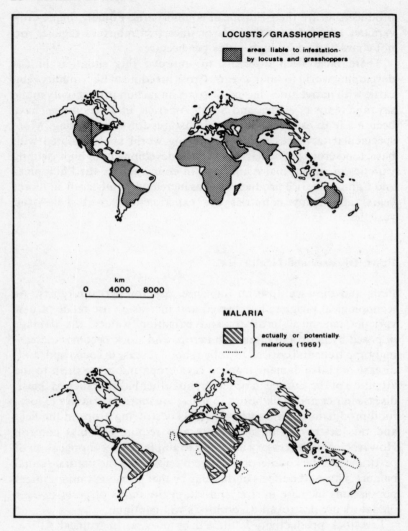

Figure 3   Areas liable to infestation by locusts/grasshoppers and areas actually or potentially malarious

but the rate of progress is affected by the character of the local population involved. Physical status and cultural attitudes are critical, in that the nutritional status of a population affects its physical activity and initiative, and hence its capacity for development. The energy requirements of an active person vary in accordance with body weight, temperature and workload. But in developing countries the calorie intake of many people is below the required minimum. Recent calculations for India suggest that a quarter of its population is in this category. Protein deficiencies also occur, especially among children, in areas where low protein crops such as cassava, yam or sweet potato form the staple diet. Elsewhere, apparent protein deficiency is associated with inadequate calorie intake which limits protein assimilation in the body. The United Nations Food and Agriculture Organization indicates that areas of greatest dietary deficiency include the 'Andean countries, the semi-arid stretches of Africa and the Near East, and some densely populated countries of Asia'.

Illness and disease also affect the level of activity of a population, with dietary deficiencies somewhat to blame in increasing human susceptibility to illness. The danger of disease remains relatively high in developing countries, because control measures, especially in the humid tropics where disease-bearing organisms flourish readily, are inadequate. Maladies range from measles and influenza, which severely affect isolated indigenous populations, to the more widespread dangers of malaria, dysentery, tuberculosis and cholera. Even in countries where progress has been made in combating such diseases, continuous vigilance is necessary. Reports from Vietnam indicate that water-filled bomb craters have provided excellent breeding grounds for malarial mosquitoes. Elsewhere comparable disruption or maladministration of prevention services can create a resurgence of disease. How far climatic conditions may also affect human activity is less clear. Hot and humid climates are commonly considered to be enervating but the assumption that they substantially reduce activity levels must be viewed with caution. Where poor health or inappropriate cultural adaptation already prevail, a tropical climate may well aggravate man's capacity for physical and mental achievement.

Cultural Limitations

Cultural factors can be a severe impediment to the development process. In rural areas, for example, the modification of traditional agricultural systems has run into difficulties because of apparent

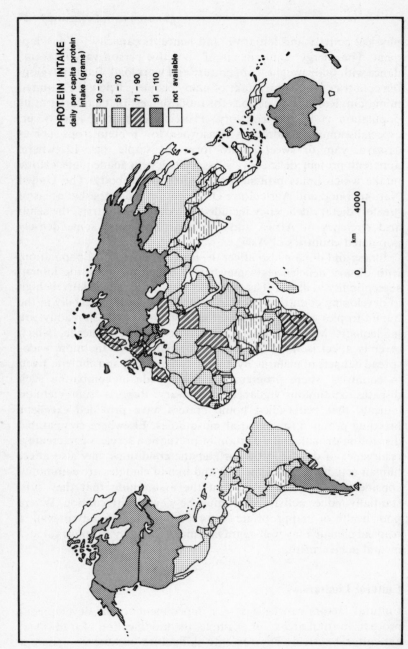

Figure 4 Global daily *per capita* protein intake

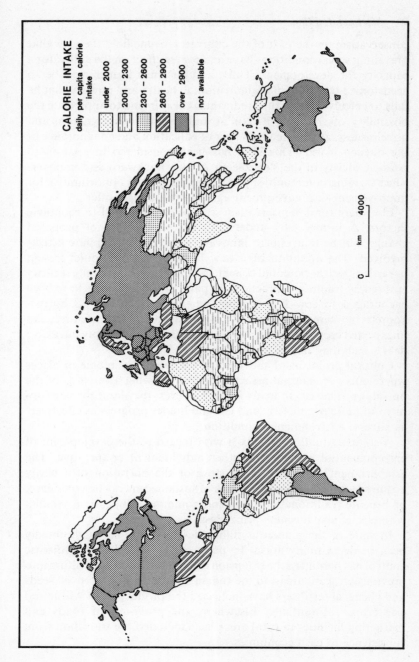

Figure 5 Global daily *per capita* calorie intake

conservatism on the part of the cultivator. Some hold the view that prevailing social conditions have an adverse effect on the cultivator's capacity for development. Thus, a subsistence farmer may be so accustomed to a state of malnutrition, ill health and poverty that he fails to perceive clearly the predicament he is in and to appreciate the possibility of changing it. His attitude is one of resignation and hopelessness, aggravated by a lack of education and an ignorance of the outside world. This view has been considered in relation to peasant society in the Venezuelan Andes. Backward and impoverished farming communities persist in spite of the opportunities for improvement that government agricultural services offer.

Elsewhere rural 'conservatism' can be more related to economic factors. A farmer may understand the implications of proposed change, but be reluctant to innovate because of the apparent risks involved. The adoption of a new land use system could present hazards as well as potential benefit and undermine the family security ensured by traditional practices. In parts of India farmers have been encouraged to sow high-yielding cereal varieties and to borrow appreciable sums for the cost of inputs on a few hectares. An unexpected crop failure means not only loss of food supply but also a debt which may take years to pay off.

Cultural problems of this kind are generally overcome in places where effective external assistance and a growing awareness of the outside world exist. In many areas, however, they limit the development of more productive land use and hinder progress as effectively as adverse environmental conditions.

A similar situation may exist with regard to the development of entrepreneurial activities, whether individual or cooperative. The establishment of a local trade store or the operation of a newly acquired lorry can founder for lack of sustained energy or experience, or because traditional customs and communal obligations conflict with elementary business principles.

In spite of the numerous difficulties, progress has undoubtedly been made in many areas. In parts of the humid tropics disease control has permitted the extension of settlement and agriculture into previously vacant areas; in the Indian subcontinent, improved seeds and chemical fertilisers have increased the production of wheat and rice crops substantially. Elsewhere, the provision of roads and marketing facilities in rural areas has facilitated the transition from subsistence to cash economies.

Whether such advance can be maintained sufficiently rapidly over the remaining decades of this century is less certain. In many developing areas the rate of progress in *per capita* terms is severely prejudiced by population growth, and many gloomy predictions are made. Family planning would ease vastly the problem of providing food and opportunity for the inhabitants of developing countries, but opposition exists in many quarters. The answer lies in exploiting effectively global resources to support a stable human population.

Development is Effort

Whatever the steps taken to achieve adequate development, there are two basic considerations. First, development needs to be undertaken in relation to the qualities and limitations of the environment if environmental potential is to be realised and its deterioration avoided. Second, technological exploitation must be culturally appropriate if ordered progress is to be made. Such considerations are as relevant in modern urban society as in the developing countries. In the case of the latter, however, ordered interaction of culture with environment is perhaps more marginally sustained and the prospects for the future less secure. The development of poorer countries calls for enormous effort, directed not least to the appropriate management of fundamental human and environmental resources.

3
Fertile People in Infertile Lands: the Demographic Situation

John I. Clarke

There can be few literate people today who are unaware of the rapid and accelerating growth of the world's population. There were about 500 million people on earth in 1650; 1000 million in 1850; 2000 million in 1930, and 3000 million in 1960; and with the current 1.9 per cent annual growth rate by 1975 the world population had risen to 4000 million. About 71 per cent of this enormous total live in the less-developed countries (LDCs) which account also for 86 per cent of present population growth. Thus, by the year 2000 they will contain more than three-quarters of the world's inhabitants.

Most LDCs have had inadequate censuses or sample enumerations and have no reliable system of vital registration, owing to illiteracy, insufficient infrastructures, suspicion of enumerations and high costs. Quality of data is therefore suspect. In some countries like Lebanon and Ethiopia, census-taking has been impeded by religious divisions, while in Nigeria the political implications of the 1962, 1963 and 1973 censuses reduced their accuracy and nullified their value. Several LDCs, other than Lebanon and Ethiopia, have never held a national census: the Somali Republic, Republic of Yemen, People's Democratic Republic of Yemen, Afghanistan and Vietnam. The nation with the world's largest population, China, has not had a census since 1953, and although the UN estimate for 1975 was 839 million other estimates varied by 200 million. However, as part of the World Population Year (1974) programmes the United Nations assisted 30 LDCs to take censuses – 20 of them for the first time.

It is often forgotten that the really large LDC populations are in Asia, and that China, India, Indonesia, Pakistan and Bangladesh together comprise 43 per cent of the total population of the world. China alone has more people than the three southern continents,

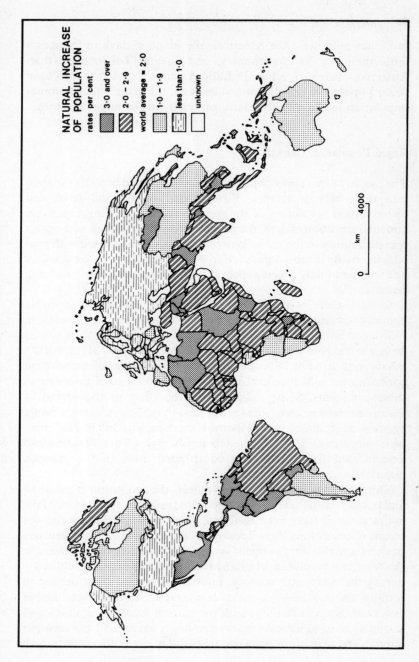

Figure 6 Rates of natural increase of world population for 1970–2

NATURAL INCREASE
OF POPULATION

rates per cent

3·0 and over

2·0 – 2·9

world average = 2·0

1·0 – 1·9

less than 1·0

unknown

0   4000
km

India has more than the Americas, the island of Java in Indonesia more than any African country, and Greater Tokyo more than Australia. Moreover, although Latin America and Africa both have faster population growth rates than Asia, the great bulk of annual population increase is of Asians, especially in the large countries.

Rapid Population Growth

The causes of this rapid population growth may be broadly grouped into three sets of factors. First, there was the industrial and technological revolution of the western world involving expansion and intensification of agriculture, increasing urbanisation and a great transformation in the use of power resources. This started with coal which initially localised population and proceeded to gas, electricity and oil, gradually freeing people from some of their localising constraints.

Second, there is the dramatic spread of Europeans to other continents, conquering, opening up, and developing 'new worlds' in North and South America, Australia, parts of Africa and inner Asia. Before this expansion took place, more than four-fifths of the world's inhabitants lived in Europe and Asia, a pattern of population concentration which reflected the long evolution of civilisations in these continents. Some indication of the effect of the spread of Europeans may be seen from the fact that in 1650 there were probably only about 15 million people living in the Americas, but in 1977 there were more than 575 million. Obviously not all are of European descent, but Europeans have contributed most to this massive population growth.

Third, rapid population growth reflects the revolution in medicine and public health that has occurred since the last century. Most of the major diseases have been analysed, their causes identified and the means of controlling them developed, and at the same time there has been remarkable improvement in sanitation and hygiene. Initiated in the West, this revolution brought about a gradual decline in mortality during the nineteenth century, later accompanied by a decline in fertility. Slowly, the subsequent 'demographic transition' resulted in low mortality and fertility, and low natural increase. In developed countries natural increase rates have rarely exceeded 1 per cent per annum, and many European countries today have either zero growth or natural decrease: Austria, Belgium, East Germany, West Germany, United Kingdom and Luxemburg. In addition, the process of demographic transition has meant profound changes in population structures, notably the evolution of the small family system and the ageing of population.

Much of the present world population growth results from the diffusion of the revolution in medicine and public health to the Third World, especially since the Second World War. This has led to a dramatic decline in the death rates of LDCs, as yet mostly unaccompanied by any substantial change is birth rates so that rates of natural increase of population have soared well above those of developed countries. Almost invariably natural increase has exceeded 1.8 per cent per annum, and occasionally reached 4 per cent in Middle America where mortality decline has been most impressive. The model of demographic transition in LDCs has a more compressed time scale than in developed countries, but the completion of demographic transition depends very much on the rate and timing of fertility decline. At the present time there are many variations in the stage of fertility and mortality decline in the Third World.

Mortality decline has been much more general than fertility decline, but the varied stages in this process reached by LDCs leave a patchwork map of world death rates. As fertility is usually high, the level of mortality in LDCs is often the main determinant of their rates of population growth. Some have death rates well below 10 per 1000, lower than most advanced countries, and this applies particularly to many small countries and islands such as Mauritius, Reunion, Hong Kong, Singapore, Taiwan, Trinidad, Puerto Rico, Kuwait, Israel and Cyprus. In small countries like these it is not too difficult to reduce death rates, which may plunge as low as 5 per 1000, much lower than in more developed countries.

Mortality decline in LDCs is facilitated by youthful age structures, which are made even more youthful by mortality decline because this applies mostly to infants and children. Many LDCs, therefore, are now experiencing large increases in the proportion of children in their populations, and nearly all display strongly marked juvenility. More than 40 per cent of the inhabitants are normally under 15 years of age, in contrast with a maximum of 30 per cent in most developed countries. These very high proportions of young people have immense repercussions upon the economy: they increase consumption vastly but add little to production and mean high

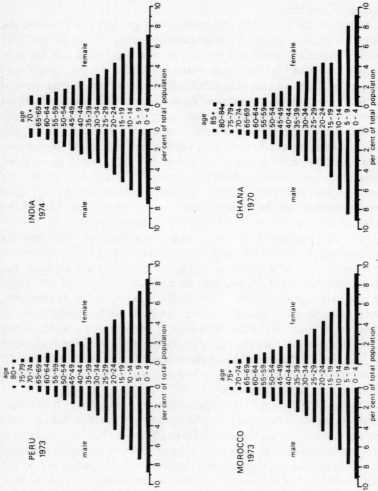

Figure 7 Age and sex distribution for Peru, India, Morocco and Ghana (in per cent of total population)

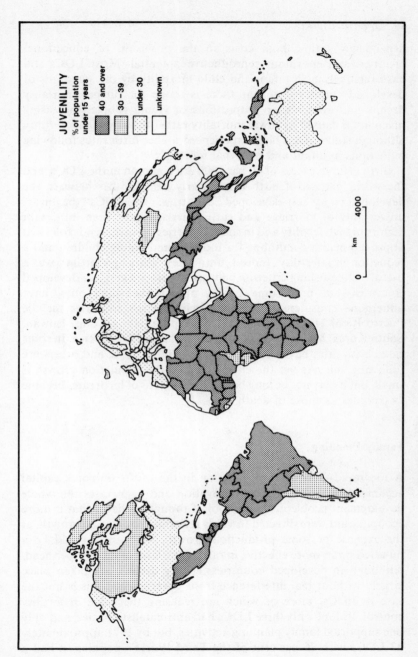

Figure 8   Percentage of world population under the age of 15

JUVENILITY
% of population
under 15 years

40 and over
30 – 39
under 30
unknown

0   4000
        km

dependency ratios, high costs in the provision of educational facilities, and enormous reproductive potential. Most LDCs still have relatively high infant and child mortality by the standards of developed countries so that there is scope for further mortality decline and even higher proportions of young people. Increasing juvenility is caused by lower mortality rather than by higher fertility although some LDCs have experienced higher birth rates following reductions in infant and maternal mortality.

Birth rates in excess of 40 per 1000 are common in the LDCs, and the world pattern of birth rates clearly distinguishes between the developed and less-developed countries. In LDCs the near-universality of marriage and early marriage have been important factors in high fertility and in some countries upward trends followed improved health conditions for mothers and young children and a reduction in infertility. Indeed, until a few years ago fertility was a useful distinguishing criterion between developed and less-developed countries, but now some LDCs, mainly the small ones, have undergone considerable fertility decline. Such countries include Puerto Rico, Trinidad, Malaysia, Singapore, Hong Kong, Taiwan, South Korea, Mauritius, Cyprus, Sri Lanka and Costa Rica. In some cases birth rates have descended below 30 per 1000, and others are following suit. As yet the effect upon world population growth is small, but it may not be long before the patterns of birth rates become as complex as those of death rates.

Family Planning

A too rapid increase in population in the LDCs outpaces capital accumulation and technical innovation and aggravates the whole development problem. One school of thought believes that if more economic aid were directed towards retarding population growth, at the expense of some production growth, the money could be a hundred times more effective in raising the level of income per head. Although in developed countries fertility decline has taken place largely without real interference from governments, this is not the case in LDCs, more of which are realising the value of fertility control. In 1960 only three LDCs had anti-natalist policies, and only one supported family planning activities, but by 1971 approximately 33 LDCs with 76 per cent of the Third World's population had a population policy or programme, and 31 others supported family planning. The real effect of this impressive advance is still limited, because official support does not necessarily mean intensive programmes. Overall effectiveness is very difficult to analyse for there are few reliable data on fertility and other factors such as changing mortality and abstention and abortion in birth control, both common in the Third World, may be involved. Unfortunately, progress in family planning in some LDCs has been retarded by the unpopularity of intra-uterine devices and future success largely depends on developments in contraceptive technology. Surveys reveal that women in LDCs now want fewer children; the number desired is usually greater than in developed countries but less than would have been normal in pre-birth control times. There are, however, marked national and cultural variations in desired family size, and governments can only succeed in reducing fertility by changing socio-economic levels and aspirations so that a reduced family size is desirable. Contraceptive technology alone is not enough.

Continental variations occur in the attitudes of governments and peoples to family planning. The governments of India, China, Pakistan, Indonesia, Sri Lanka, South Korea, the Philippines, Taiwan, Malaysia, Singapore and Nepal are making serious efforts to reduce birth rates. In Hong Kong the crude birth rate has declined from about 35 to 20 per 1000 over a period of 10 years, initially through a change in age structure and marital status. From 1966 there was also a reduction in the fertility of married women. The South Korean birth rate also fell by about ten points to 24 per 1000 by the mid 1970s because of later marriage, increased frequency of induced abortion and the fact that half the married women in the reproductive age groups now practise contraception. Many emigrant Chinese communities in other Asian countries are experiencing fertility decline and there are reasonable grounds to assume that in China itself — despite ambivalent attitudes toward family planning — later marriage, birth control and a growing stigma against large families are reducing fertility substantially. Some experts place the birth rate of China as low as 27 per 1000 and such a dramatic reduction would have a profound effect upon world population growth; at the moment this is largely offset by a reduction in mortality.

Progress in family planning is much more limited in Africa and

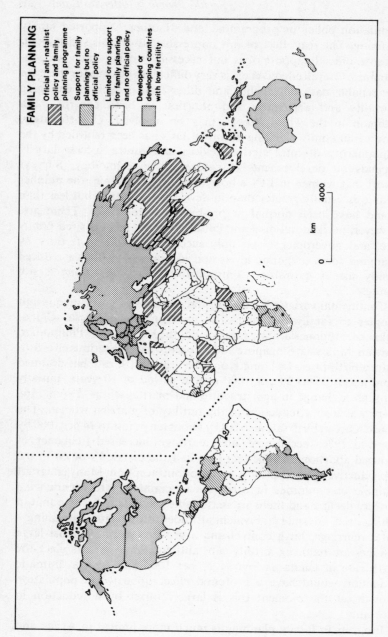

Figure 9 Family planning

FAMILY PLANNING

- Official anti-natalist policy and family planning programme
- Support for family planning but no official policy
- Limited or no support for family planning and no official policy
- Developed or developing countries with low fertility

0   4000
km

Latin America than it is in Asia. Some African countries feel that population size and political status are directly related so that more people are wanted rather than fewer. Furthermore, in view of social customs and structures it is difficult for a family planning programme to get under way. The only major progress in mainland Africa has been made in Tunisia in conjunction with a number of social measures to abolish polygamy, modify the divorce laws, delay marriage and raise the status of women; but even there the birth rate still exceeds 30 per 1000.

The influence of the Roman Catholic church has impeded the spread of family planning programmes in the whole of Latin America. Their *raison d'etre* is improvement of maternal and child health and reduction in the number of abortions rather than restriction of population growth. But religious influence is far from being the only factor; prestige of male virility is certainly another. Family planning is sometimes denounced as an alien ideal or an American trick to limit the numerical superiority of the Third World, 'the only superiority they have'. Many also regard Latin American LDCs as underpopulated with large open spaces available for development, and only capable of being developed by larger numbers of people. Whether this is true or not, the important point often not realised in the West is that many people in LDCs do not accept alarmist attitudes. Some people regard the family planning movement, and conservation for that matter, with undiluted suspicion as being aimed at maintaining existing economic structures and hierarchies. The emphasis on the population problem of the Third World is supposed merely to conceal the massive economic inequalities between the rich nations and the poor, although of course most of the world's 80 million extra people each year will live among the poor.

Population Growth and Economic Growth

There are many factors other than population growth involved in the poverty and backwardness of the Third World, but it has long been assumed that rapid population growth in the developing world has nullified programmes of economic growth. More mouths mean more problems. Conversely, however, some hold that population pressure is a force powerful enough to shatter man's inherent conservatism and force him to make innovations, inventions and devices for increasing productivity. So far in the developing world there seems more evidence that a rapidly increasing population is a brake upon the speed of development, but no simple correlations have been found between population growth and economic growth during the 1950s and 1960s. It is fair to state that there is now considerable debate and controversy among experts over the whole relationship between national development and population growth.

In the agricultural communities of many LDCs pressure of population on the land has had both social and economic impact. Large estate and plantation systems have a relatively inelastic demand for labour, and the more people seeking work the greater the depression of wage levels; similarly, share-cropping tenancies become subject to harsher terms. With increasing demand the value of land rises, rents become forced up and land as a source of wealth attracts capital that would be more effective if invested in other sectors of the economy. The character of farming also responds to growing population pressure. All too often, labour-intensive methods of husbandry become inbuilt into the economy. Quality and variety are sacrificed to quantity and labour-demanding crops are favoured. The social consequences of this situation are varied, but in many countries the power and wealth of the landowning class has grown while that of the mass of the peasantry has decreased. A two-class society has arisen divided by a deep gulf which the small but growing middle, professional, and commercial class cannot yet span. This is the genesis of the surplus element in the agrarian populations that acts as a disincentive to agricultural improvement and leads to unrest, demands for land reform and even revolution.

One feature which is particularly evident to geographers is that the LDCs exhibit immense areal variations in population density and concentration, much of which are related more to past economies than to present growth rates. For example, China and India have vast numbers because of the success and longevity of their peasant civilisations more than their present natural increase. Moreover, rapid urbanisation involves more people than the colonisation of empty areas, and consequently populations are generally becoming more concentrated; this process is more advanced in Latin America and the Middle East than in tropical Africa and south Asia.

There are also marked contrasts in the relationship of population to economic development and in population pressure on resources. These are, however, extremely difficult to measure. Too often population density is considered a suitable indication of population pressure, but pressure may be high in a sparsely-populated area. Despite difficulties in finding a suitable index there are striking contrasts between the high population/resource ratios of countries such as China, Bangladesh and Egypt, and the low ratios of many countries of tropical Africa, such as Gabon and Zambia.

Population/resource ratios are not specifically affected by political boundaries but the mesh of such boundaries is important in its braking effect upon spontaneous population flows between LDCs. The Chinese have difficulty in emigrating owing to restrictions on departure and arrival; the Indians experience restrictions on arrival. But emigration certainly can have no major effects upon populations as large as these. Indeed, international migration can only play an important role in the population problems of small states such as Kuwait, Lebanon, Israel, Hong Kong, Jamaica, Puerto Rico or Lesotho, but even between the micro-states of fragmented Africa there is increasing difficulty of movement. President Amin's de-pluralisation of Uganda is one example of the nationalisation of population problems, identifiable from Bangladesh to Burundi and from China to Chile.

The diversity of the populations of LDCs makes consideration of their collective demography somewhat superficial. Any major region of the world reveals immense contrasts, inequality and inefficiency. In the Middle East there are examples of countries with large populations (Turkey) and tiny populations (United Arab Emirates); with high population pressure (Egypt) and low pressure (Libya); with high fertility (People's Democratic Republic of Yemen) and low fertility (Cyprus); with high mortality (Saudi Arabia) and low mortality (Kuwait); with populationist policies (Libya) and anti-natalist policies (Turkey); with linguistic uniformity (Saudi Arabia) and linguistic diversity (Iran); with religious uniformity (Republic of Yemen) and religious diversity (Lebanon); with a mainly urban population (Israel) and a mainly rural population (Oman); with one dominant city (Iraq) and several (Syria); with a strong emigration (Lebanon) and strong immigration (Jordan); with few foreigners (Republic of Yemen) and with a majority of them (Kuwait). Certainly the Middle East exhibits more demographic diversity than many other parts of the Third World, but it shows well that demographic models of the Third World are often over-simplistic.

Demographic diversity is even more evident within LDCs than

between them. It results partly from the persistence of traditional contrasts in ways of life and limitations upon mobility which have given rise to immense ethnic complexity. In tropical Africa and south-east Asia, for example, there are profusions of peoples and languages. Diversity also results from the highly localised and often peripheral nature of the modern economy which involves only a small proportion of the population. Mines, industries, commercial agriculture and cities with a growing concentration of services, facilities and amenities have become centres of lower mortality, higher natural increase and attraction for migrants. This has intensified disparities in regional development particularly where there is strong alien implantation, as of Chinese in Malaysia or of Europeans in Rhodesia. Consequently the population distributions of many LDCs tend to be very uneven, and with the rapid growth of one or two large cities population concentration becomes excessive, as in Thailand, Philippines, Sri Lanka, Senegal, Mexico and Peru. Unfortunately, although such patterns of population distribution are far from ideal, LDCs are often encouraged to give more thought to population growth than distribution. Brazil, China and Tanzania, however, have made deliberate attempts to reduce the external orientation and coastal concentration of their people, but it is not easy to change population patterns by government planning. Population numbers are not easy to control, at any level.

The Third World is undoubtedly in a stage of very rapid demographic transition. Already there are changes in mortality and mobility in most countries and soon there will be much more widespread fertility decline. Without this, population growth rates of LDCs will remain high or become even higher because there is still scope and hope for further control of mortality. These problems weigh heavily on development planners in the production of a strategy for development.

4
Economic Planning: Paths to Development

Colin R. Patman

More than 1450 national development plans have been published in the countries of the Third World, but despite twenty-five years of research into the theory of development, approaches to social and economic progress remain characteristically unrealistic. All too frequently planned targets have not been achieved suggesting that even more research is required before effective development guidelines will be available to Third World development planners.

The creation of an adequate theoretical and institutional framework for planned economic and social development has been and still is the task of academics from a variety of disciplines, not least economists and geographers. Many now accept that the swiftest way to economic development is the organisation of the complete resources of a state, and that plans should be aimed at increasing a country's productive powers as well as obtaining the necessary capital for investment. Inevitably, governments have had to take on the role of the central administrative authority, and decide total capital requirements, investment strategy, and from where domestic and foreign finance is to be obtained. The economic theories behind such government planning and the character of the plans actually adopted have changed greatly during the period since the Second World War.

Although LDCs have been a focus of concern over recent decades, economists working during the early part of this century were predominantly involved in the problems of the developed world. Their object was to plan for economic stability at home, to redress the massive imbalance between the supply and demand for labour and other resources. Economic growth in both the developed and the undeveloped world remained a secondary issue. Economists who did consider the less-developed world appear to have assumed, like Karl Marx, that 'the more developed society presents to the less developed society a picture of its own future'. The LDCs did not therefore merit special attention.

It was not until the 1950s that the validity of the assumption that all countries must ultimately follow a similar path of development was seriously challenged. The gap between the rich and the poor countries was dramatically widening and the political strength of the latter was growing fast. The social, demographic and geographical realities of the contemporary Third World could be disregarded no longer.

It is only during the past few years that geographers have made any real contribution to the solution of Third World problems. Traditionally, they have drawn attention to the geographical uniqueness of the individual countries, a contrast to the common denominators, key factors and regularities in the development process sought by the economic theorists who have so far been responsible for most of the literature. But this divergence in viewpoint is narrowing with both sides adopting less extreme positions. They have not succeeded in constructing a general theory of development but have established a partial framework.

Capital and its Employment

There is a further difference of opinion concerning the importance of capital against the importance of the part played by national resources, especially natural resources. Geographers have been criticised for emphasising the degree of resource endowment: the quantity and quality of land, mineral deposits, sources of power. And yet there is no doubt that the almost complete lack of resources or the exploitation of one major resource has a profound impact on the character and rate of economic growth. In the mid 1950s few could have predicted the development potential of Libya. Its land is almost all desert or semi-desert. In 1954 Libya's population was only 1.1 million, with one of the lowest *per capita* incomes in the world. A dramatic change followed the discovery of oil. Production began in September 1961, and annual oil exports had reached over a million barrels by 1969. Revenue from oil enabled the government to raise its expenditure from a mere 22.7 million in 1961 to a planned expenditure of $5085 million in 1977. Although a nation's average *per capita* income is a notoriously poor indicator of living standards or level of development, by 1976 the figure for Libya was in excess of $5100. Wealth has not only brought political power, but there are signs of expansion in other economic sectors, for example in food processing and cement production. It still remains to be seen whether the concentration of capital investment in the oil industry will have a widespread impact on the rest of the economy. Mass production will be delayed or may even be prevented by the small size of the labour force, estimated to be 466000 in 1970. The demand for consumer durable goods has risen. Total vehicle registrations, for example, were over 15000 in 1970 but this has led to an increase in imports rather than a transformation of the traditional economy.

The Libyan story is not characteristic of many countries outside the Organisation of Petroleum Exporting Countries (OPEC). There is not a very close correlation between known resources and wealth or gross national product (GNP) in the Third World. Many economists have argued that the critical relationship is not between resources and wealth, but between capital and output. GNP is said to depend directly on two factors: the relationship between real capital and output, and the volume of capital utilised. The capital/output ratio is at the very core of economic planning policy. It refers to the increase in capital investment required to increase real output by one unit. It may be applied as a ratio for the entire economy or it may refer to a particular sector of the economy. In general an increase of overall output by one unit requires an input of three or four times as much capital, 3:1 or 4:1. However, in some sectors, such as heavy industries, the vast requirement of overhead capital in the form of machinery, power supplies and transport facilities, gives a much higher and less attractive ratio which may be double the national average, 6:1 to 8:1 or more. Investment in agriculture tends to yield more favourable returns, possibly approaching 1:1. Thus, the rate of economic growth depends not only on the volume of financial resources invested but on how it is invested.

Architects of many of the early development plans discovered that substantial capital investment in basic industry did not necessarily secure high rates of economic growth. In Pakistan, for example, it was anticipated that the First Five-Year Plan, 1955–60, would raise national income by over 15 per cent. In spite of a gross underestimate of the volume of private investment, national income rose by a rather disappointing 12 per cent. This was partly the result of an investment programme which largely ignored the agricultural sector and emphasised heavy industry, such as the chemical industries and power production, where capital/output ratios are high. The forecasts were over-optimistic but this does not necessarily mean that the investment 'mix' was distorted. In the initial stages of planning the growth rate is probably not as significant as the structural change. Moreover capital/output ratios are likely to change. In the short run, during the

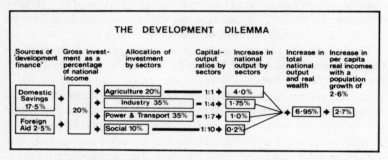

Figure 10   Relationship between investment and development

First, or even the Second, Five-Year Plan investment in infrastructure and basic industry may yield a low return. In the longer term, the fuller utilisation of agricultural, industrial and labour resources that results may dramatically reduce capital/output ratios. In Pakistan, by 1965, at the end of the Second Five-Year Plan, there were signs of just such a trend, in spite of agriculture continuing to receive relatively low priority with but 15 per cent of total development expenditure.

It is easy to criticise the early plans and to claim that the more recent emphasis on agriculture, on the green rather than the industrial revolution, admits to the wrong investment 'mix'. But the sheer urgency of their problems forced many countries to proceed with their plans before they were able to collect and assemble adequate data. Even now, more work needs to be done both to improve the accuracy of capital/output forecasting and to obtain more satisfactory information concerning the nature of the Third World's resources. The latter must be the contribution of the geographer and far from abandoning his traditional approach it would seem appropriate that he should pursue it. The capital and the resource approaches have neither failed nor succeeded in explaining or promoting the process of development. They have highlighted the inadequacy of existing techniques especially in the forecasting of output and in the evaluation of resources.

A third difference of viewpoint on the process of development lies in the value of identifying the stages of economic growth through time rather than the pattern of development on the ground within national boundaries. Here the division is not primarily between geographers and economists.

W. W. Rostow, writing in 1956, was concerned with stages of growth in time, and found that economic growth is not a continuous progression. He identified three phases: a long period when the preconditions for 'take-off' are established, a critical period of between 20 and 30 years when take-off occurs, and a subsequent long but indefinite period when growth becomes relatively automatic. His analysis of a number of developed nations led him to believe that a necessary but not sufficient, condition for take-off is a rate of net investment equivalent to at least 10 per cent of national income. The process by which a community changes from a 5 per cent to a 10 per cent investor can usually be traced to a particularly sharp stimulus such as the development of one or more substantial manufacturing industries with a high rate of growth, or to the emergence of a political, social and institutional framework with the ability to exploit existing potential. In the United States between 1840 and 1860 the stimuli were a sharp relative increase in export prices, large capital imports and the technical innovation associated with the construction of the railroads. Rostow considered Mexico, Brazil, Argentina, and Turkey to be in their take-off states in the mid 1950s.

Many authorities have criticised Rostow's work. They have pointed out that distinct stages are in many cases impossible to identify. In Colombia, for example, studies by the United Nations and others have confirmed that although technological and economic progress has been erratic, in general it has been fairly steady since the spread of coffee cultivation in the 1860s. Rostow's model may not have a universal application but unlike so many economists he did at least examine specific countries and few geographers could quarrel with his conclusion that 'in the end "take-off" requires that a society find a way to apply effectively its own peculiar resources'.

Dual Economies and Regional Balance

Some economists and planners have been less sympathetic to the geographical viewpoint. Planning designed to promote development outside the existing major centres of activity is said to have the effect of reducing the efficiency of resource utilisation. Throughout the Third World this view has led to the creation of dual economies. One or two developed core areas are surrounded by extensive undeveloped areas. Intense dualism may be economically efficient in the early stages of development but it has put the many inhabitants of undeveloped areas beyond their own trading economy. In the long run this may constrain national growth by reducing the size of the domestic consumer market.

The process by which dual economies are created was described by G. Myrdal in 1957. He pointed out that the early stages of development are normally accompanied by a 'backwash effect'. This is the process by which labour, capital, enterprise, domestic monopoly power, and social and economic infrastructure gravitate towards the major growth areas. In the Third World these areas constitute a characteristically small proportion of national territory. He also identified 'a spread effect' by suggesting that in the long term the prosperous area's capacity to provide goods and services will be outstripped by the expansion of the domestic market. Moreover, it will ultimately suffer congestion and shortages of land and labour, which further stimulate the spread effect.

Continuing dualism is a common feature of many less-developed countries. In Uganda, for example, the rapid development of the Kampala and Jinja regions appears to have created considerable backwash effects in the poorer northern and western regions. In Pakistan during the 1960s, the movement of capital from the lagging East to the more prosperous cities of the West contributed to the increased disparity in average income between East and West, from 20 per cent in 1959 to 40 per cent in 1968. Dualism of this order is not excessive when compared with that of many other countries, but there is little doubt that it was an important factor in the political upheaval which led to the creation of Bangladesh. The reduction of regional economic and social inequalities now occupies an important place in the strategy of an increasing number of national development plans.

In Latin America where the problem has received the most

attention, dualism is probably the most dominant feature of its economic and social geography. For example the migration of capital and population to São Paulo and Rio de Janeiro have created such intensive 'backwash' that by 1967 approximately three-quarters of Brazil's manufacturing and service industries were concentrated in these centres. Buenos Aires, Mexico City, Lima/Callao and Santiago/Valparaiso have assumed similar economic importance in their respective countries.

Some economists, notably A. Hirschman, have claimed that in the absence of government intervention 'backwash', or 'polarisation' as he terms it, will continue indefinitely as an inevitable accompaniment to economic expansion. If this is so, planners cannot afford to take the long-term view or simply sit back and wait for spread to take place 'naturally'. It is significant that reducing regional, economic and social inequalities has come to occupy an important place in the strategy of an increasing number of national plans.

The problem of the lagging region is often approached through development of the 'resource frontier' and agricultural development schemes. One of the most notable resource frontier developments is in north-east Venezuela at Santo Tome de Guayana. The Guayana Development Corporation was established to convert a resource frontier based on iron ore, iron- and steel-making capacity and hydroelectric power into an integrated and comprehensive programme of regional development. Few current national plans omit to mention regional agricultural projects and the examples are legion, from massive irrigation schemes like the Indus Basin Plan to the more modest proposals. An example is the development of the Kufra of Libya by means of the irrigation of up to 100000 hectares of hitherto unproductive land.

Planners must remember, however, that unless there are substantial unused resources, as in Venezuela, investment in existing progressive, rather than lagging, regions is likely to yield the greatest returns in the short term. The concentration of economic activity in certain districts can maximise the uses for local power supplies or nationally scarce transport facilities. This does not preclude policies designed to redress regional imbalance but planners need to recognise that such policies take time to bear fruit and that longer-term benefits have to be weighed against short-term costs.

Structural Balance

The problem of regional balance is paralleled by one of structural balance. Fierce controversy has raged around this question. Advocates of 'balanced growth' point out that structural bottlenecks reduce overall growth and that this means that all sectors of the economy should therefore be expanded at approximately the same rate. It is no good expanding the industrial sector and neglecting the agricultural sector because additional income will simply be spent on imported agricultural products and a balance of payments problem and a constraint on growth will follow. A. Lewis, arguing that industry, agriculture and infrastructure should be developed simultaneously has claimed that 'less-developed countries have not handled this aspect of their affairs adequately'.

The advocates of 'unbalanced growth' argue that an LDC will optimise growth if investment is concentrated in those sectors particularly suited for development. These sectors will be determined by existing and potential combination of resources available. Attention is also focused on the creation of viable enterprises associated with the concentration of investment and advantages of large-scale production. Imbalance is therefore a necessary (although not sufficient) condition of efficiency. A. O. Hirschman urges LDCs to follow a path of unbalanced growth and suggests another reason. He argues that investment will receive its sharpest stimulus from the very shortages and bottlenecks deplored by others. Development is seen as a series of mainly short, sharp processes designed to redress in part imbalances and to create new ones – 'each move in the sequence is induced by a previous disequilibrium and in turn creates a new disequilibrium that requires a further move'.

The debate remains largely unresolved but in recent years planners seem to have avoided either extreme by emphasising sectional integration rather than balance or imbalance. Integration is more than the establishment of the right mix between balanced and unbalanced growth. There are dynamic relationships between sectors, and integrated planning demands that these are understood and investment directed so that sectors support and strengthen each other. This may mean changing the nature of an activity, not merely its relative amount. Some kinds of economic growth will promote employment, others will cause unemployment. A major preoccupation of the planners is therefore the analysis of the interrelationships and linkages between sectors of development. Most national development plans now include an analysis of cross-sectional studies in the form of input—output tables. It is possible to compare the output of one sector with the input requirements of sectors using that output. Disequilibria can then be identified and informed decisions taken about the need for remedial action.

Economic progress is heavily dependent on the human factor. Primary importance in planning is now being given to such factors as the adaptability of society, its attitudes to innovation and change, and to the attitudes of the traditional elite to the social and political changes which normally accompany development. For example E. E. Hagen has stressed the role of what he terms 'technological creativity' in the process of development. Technical change is seen as a function not of investment but of social, even physiological factors. At a more practical level he points out that 'so simple a tool as a spade cannot be imported into a low income society with full efficiency until the level of living has risen sufficiently that it includes the wearing of shoes'. A common problem is the desire of the political and social elite to maintain their status. This often perpetuates a feudal mentality among the mass of the population. This problem is often tackled by agrarian reform which involves the redistribution of land from the wealthy to the smallest farmers and to hitherto landless labourers. But social change is not necessarily dependent on redistribution of property. There is a well-documented case in Peru where the behaviour of the Visco Indians was radically altered by rather more subtle, social policies. The Indians were caught in the 'culture of poverty'. They were so disorganised socially that they were vulnerable to economic exploitation as agricultural labourers. In the circumstances they did not assume responsibility in public affairs and an adequate leadership did not develop. In a five-year programme the introduction of wage labour, the demonstration of new agricultural techniques and a broad policy designed to improve the nutrition, health and education of the Indians brought them within the development process. By the end of five years they had begun to assume positions of responsibility and authority and even control the *hacienda* system.

Inequality in the distribution of income is a social problem for most developing countries. However, greater equality in income may or may not reduce the resources a country can set aside for investment. If the wealthy spend their money on conspicuous consumption or on property, or if most industrial investment is in the hands of the government, income inequality will not stimulate economic growth. There is no doubt, however, that higher incomes can be an incentive to higher production, acquisition of new skills and upward social mobility. But where rigid social systems exist, differences in wealth are regarded apathetically among low income groups who have no hope of self-improvement. Inevitably, published development plans claim to promote 'social justice', but attempts to promote industrialisation through fiscal incentives and investment grants frequently result in substantial subsidies to the wealthy.

Unfortunately, inadequate data and measurement techniques still prevent the systematic integration of social and economic policies in development planning. Satisfactory indicators of such services as health, education, and social security are still lacking. Some aspects of the quality of life, such as freedom of choice, cannot be measured at all. Given that planning involves the distribution of scarce resources it is still virtually impossible to assess the value of social expenditure. It is highly probable, although difficult to demonstrate objectively, that national planners have tended to allocate insufficient funds to the social sector. In 1960 Indonesia was estimated to have the highest number of inhabitants per physician in Asia, approximately 29 500 people to every doctor compared with 6200 in Pakistan. Nevertheless, Indonesia's Five-Year Plan, 1969–73, allocated only $1 billion to health and family planning out of a total expenditure of $25 billion. Since 1973 net export earnings from oil have risen from $399 million to a budgeted $4656 million for 1978–9. Social expenditure has risen almost proportionately but the Jakarta squatter settlements remain and in spite of a recent annual growth rate of 7 per cent, unemployment and underemployment amount to 40 per cent of the labour force.

In the next decade of development it seems unlikely that the Third World will benefit from any radical changes in the theoretical basis of planning. The basic issues and alternatives are known and tried. Detailed research into the successes and failures of past plans and the practical experience gained by both the planners and the communities they serve will however assume increasing value. Such experience will at least allow less-developed countries to discriminate between the real and the largely academic issues and ultimately enable each country to tailor its development strategy to its own specific needs and resources.

5
The Rural Revolution

David Grigg

Most countries of the Third World have between one-half and three-quarters of their working population engaged in agriculture, and a very small proportion in industry, transport or commerce. The developed countries have less than one-tenth of their labour force in agriculture, in some cases less than one-twentieth. The conclusion too frequently drawn from this is that a poor country can only become rich by concentrating all of its resources on industrialisation, leaving the farmers, the bulk of the population, to fend for themselves.

There are two objections to this belief. First, agriculture is not simply a reservoir of labour and capital for the process of industrialisation. Many people in the LDCs still suffer from undernutrition, many more from malnutrition, and the populations continue to grow. More food must be forthcoming and this can only be achieved by radical institutional and technological changes. Further, for many LDCs, crops constitute the bulk of their exports, and greater efficiency in their production is essential if this income is to be maintained. Second, it is often forgotten that the developed countries all experienced remarkable changes in their farming before the first stages of industrialisation began. From the seventeenth to the nineteenth centuries the medieval institutions of Western Europe were slowly dismantled and the output of farming substantially increased. New crops such as turnips, clover and potatoes were adopted, more manure was applied and new implements used. These changes allowed agriculture to provide labour for the growing industries without any fall in total output, and indeed in some cases much of the capital for industrial investment also came from the agricultural sector. By the end of the nineteenth century the flow was reversed. Agriculture, which had sparked off industrialisation, became increasingly dependent upon industry for iron machinery,

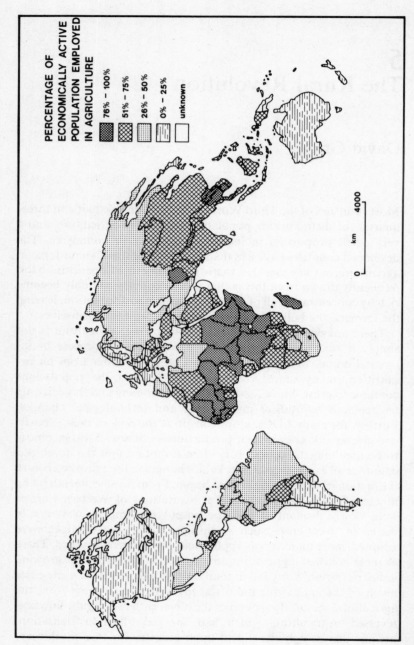

Figure 11   Percentage of workers involved in agriculture

for cheap fertilisers, and for the processing and marketing of its goods.

By the early 1960s there was a growing realisation both in the countries of the Third World and amongst their advisers that agriculture should receive more attention. Indeed, it is extraordinary how low investment was in agriculture in countries where not only was the great bulk of the population dependent on agriculture, but also much of their export income came from agricultural products. In Nigeria federal investment in agriculture rarely rose above 5 per cent of all public investment between 1949 and 1962. It was only in the 1960s that development plans substantially increased investment in agriculture. Since 1965 this has had remarkable results in some areas; the planting of new high-yield wheat and rice varieties in parts of India, Pakistan and the Philippines, together with increased use of fertiliser and irrigation have substantially increased output, and this has come to be known, perhaps a little prematurely, as the Green Revolution. The Green Revolution, though undoubtedly spectacular, has touched a minority of Asian farmers and brought problems even for them. Agriculture in the LDCs is still backward and inefficient.

Backwardness of Agriculture

The list of reasons is endless. One is farm structure: throughout most of Asia, Africa and Latin America farms are remarkably small, a few hectares at the most. In Java, for example, 86 per cent of all farms are less than 1 hectare; with increasing rural populations competing for land the average arable per farm fell from 1 hectare in 1931 to 0.66 hectares in 1961. Furthermore they are highly fragmented, being made up of fields scattered at some distance from one another. Not only does the farmer waste time moving from one plot to the next, but the layout increases the difficulties of irrigation, moving fertilisers and controlling plant diseases. Farms are in many cases so small that they cannot provide an adequate income to sustain the family, let alone allow investment in the new inputs such as fertilisers, new seeds and better implements that are essential for change. In spite of the land reform campaigns that have swept much of the Third World since 1945, there are still many farmers who rent their land from landlords on iniquitous terms; in densely-populated countries with many landless labourers, exorbitant rents can be charged. Not only is the farmer unable to save enough to improve his farm, but he often has to borrow to buy the essentials of everyday life. Interest rates are high and farmers are soon enmeshed in a spiral of debt. Also, in parts of Africa and Asia it is not tenancy that inhibits the spirit of enterprise, but the persistence of communal tenure where the individual is unlikely to put energy or capial into new methods.

Many farmers are still semi-subsistent, that is, their first concern is to provide food for their family and perhaps a small surplus to pay taxes. They are relatively unresponsive to price changes. In many cases farmers are physically isolated from the market. Poor transport conditions mean cash crops cannot be usefully grown; this limits income, investment and improvement. Some writers discount the importance of economic factors in agricultural change and emphasise social problems stressing, for example, how the prevalence of the extended family and tribal custom preclude individual enterprise; how religious attitudes limit the proper exploitation of livestock; and perhaps most important, how lack of education limits the farmer's horizon and makes him reluctant to change established methods. Thus, attempts to improve livestock kept by the Masai in East Africa have foundered because they and many other African pastoralists keep cattle for the prestige which accrues to sheer numbers; any improvement must adjust cattle numbers to the grazing resources available. The Masai are reluctant to cull their animals so that overgrazing, soil erosion and a further reduction of grazing resources continues.

There are however some good reasons for many traditional farmers' reluctance to change their methods. Living near to the margins of subsistence, they have evolved a system of farming which guarantees a harvest in all but the most disastrous of years. To experiment introduces an element of risk, and the penalty of failure is not merely a loss of income but possibly starvation. Many writers have argued that, given the factors of production at their disposal, traditional farmers are remarkably efficient in their allocation of resources. They can only raise their productivity if new factors are introduced – new varieties of seed, commercial fertilisers and more efficient implements.

The significance of the physical environment must not be over-looked. It is perhaps difficult for people in Britain to believe that the

British climate provides good conditions for farming. Winters are rarely long enough to limit crop growth, droughts are rare, and above all rainfall does not vary greatly from year to year. But many Asian and African farmers are constant victims of drought. Where rainfall is low, as it is in much of Africa, total annual rainfall is concentrated in one short part of the year. Not only does the amount received vary greatly from one year to another, but the date at which the rains, and thus the agricultural year, begin is uncertain. Late arrival of the rains means that the preparation of the soil has to be carried out very rapidly, at a time of the year when the food supplies from the last harvest are at a low ebb and many of the farmers are undernourished. Below-average rainfall can greatly reduce the yield of the harvest, and in the drier margins of cultivation, a run of abnormally dry years is not uncommon, as was found in the Great Plains of the United States in the 1930s and in the Sahel zone of West Africa more recently. In the Indian subcontinent rainfall is, apparently, much greater, but the monsoons are prone to great variations in the amount of rain they bring and in the time they arrive. Below-average monsoons have an obvious effect on harvests but it should not be forgotten that above-average rainfall may cause floods that can destroy harvests in the rivers and deltas where much of India's population lives. The failure of the monsoon in 1965 and 1966 undoubtedly had a retrogressive effect on the second Indian Five-Year Plan.

Nearer the equator, in the humid tropics of the Amazon basin, the Zaïre basin and the Malaysian archipelago, the growth of the natural vegetation, the tropical rainforest, is so exuberant that it would seem to be the ideal environment for crop growth. Yet outside the lower rivers and deltas, where wet rice cultivation is the major farming system, farmers have found it very difficult to crop the land continuously. Plant foods constantly move in a closed nutrient cycle, from soil to trees and, as the trees die, back to the soil. Once the forest has been cleared permanently and the soil is exposed to high temperatures and heavy rainfall, not only are many of the bases leached away, but the risk of soil erosion is greater. In the past this has been overcome by bush fallowing. Small patches of land are cleared for crops, but after two or three years the land is left and the natural vegetation allowed to regenerate. But as population has grown, the fallow periods – formerly twenty years or more – have become shorter and shorter, and it has been difficult to maintain soil fertility. Nor would it seem, if recent research is correct, that the equatorial regions are well-endowed climatically: studies of potential photo-synthesis suggest that these regions are always likely to give lower yields than the sub-tropics, where there is less cloud and a greater light intensity.

Remedial Measures

Two changes must take place if these problems are to be overcome. First, a better social and economic framework must be provided for the farmer to work in. Land reform was once thought to be the key to increasing agricultural productivity, endorsing the belief that the farmer who owns his land is more likely to adopt new methods than the farmer who has to give half his harvest to the landlord and much of the rest to the local money-lender. Desirable though land reform may be, it does not necessarily make the farmer a better farmer and many land reform schemes have had disappointing results. Similarly farm size: if farms are too small they should be amalgamated. But what happens to the dispossessed, and the rapidly growing rural populations without land? There are few jobs for them in the towns, and far from creating bigger and more efficient farms, many governments have put a limit on sizes of holdings to try to ensure that everyone has some land.

Great hopes were placed on the building of roads and railways. They were expected to shatter the structure of traditional society, drag the farmer into the market place, and encourage efficiency. But once the Afro-Asian farmer finds his way to the world market the prospects are gloomy. Prices for agricultural products are notoriously unstable, and are declining in the long term *vis-a-vis* the goods that the LDCs want to buy.

The second part of the problem lies on the farm itself. Most peasant farming systems are efficient, given the environmental and economic conditions within which they have evolved. But to secure the great increases in productivity that are necessary, quite new inputs must be obtained. However, there have been fashions in technological panaceas. Until the early 1960s there was a widespread belief that mechanisation, which was the basis of modern agriculture in North America and to a lesser extent in Western Europe, would solve the problem. Only slowly was it realised that the introduction of combine harvesters and caterpillar tractors had little relevance for small farmers. An 'intermediate' technology which can bridge the gap between the primitive implements of many farmers and the sophisticated machinery of the West is needed. European farmers themselves did not change overnight from sickles and flails to combine harvesters and in the nineteenth century marked advances in productivity were obtained by replacing the sickle with the scythe, and then the scythe with the reaper.

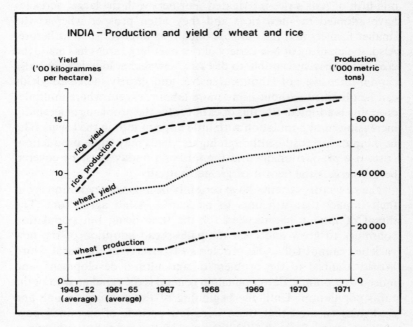

Figure 12   Production and yield of wheat and rice in India, 1948–71

At present, farmers and governments are looking not to labour-saving devices but to methods of obtaining higher yields per hectare. At the centre of the Green Revolution are the new hybrid wheat and rice varieties. Hybrids are obtained by cross-breeding genetically unlike varieties of the same plant, and the aims are higher yields, and more rapid maturity. The first hybrid corn was produced commercially in the United States in the 1920s, and by the 1960s it had almost entirely replaced traditional varieties. After the Second World War, experiments in hybrid wheats proved successful in Mexico. A commercial hybrid rice was bred in the Philippines which began to be grown more widely in 1966; it not only gives higher yields than traditional rices, but the shorter growing season allows the spread of multiple cropping.

Outside the Philippines, however, comparatively few farmers have adopted the new rice varieties developed by the International Rice Research Institute there. Hybrids are high-yielding, but only if given ample fertiliser and irrigation water. Fertiliser is expensive, and only one-fifth of Asia's rice is irrigated. Farmers with the larger acreages have adopted the new rices and they often prosper whereas the smaller farmers and the landless remain as impoverished as before. Also, the planting of one variety of rice over large areas has made the crop singularly susceptible to disease. New technology is essentially capital-intensive not labour-intensive, and greatly increased yields can be obtained without using more labour, except where multiple-cropping is adopted. But this does not solve the problems of a rapidly increasing rural population with little hope of jobs in the towns. The new inputs are costly; although higher yields may triple production, costs rise proportionally and the farmer's outlay must be covered before he gets the benefit of greater output.

The new crop varieties have certainly been more revolutionary in their impact than attempts to mechanise Asian agriculture. The threat of famine has receded for the time being but population continues to grow and even the widespread adoption of the new varieties cannot solve the problems of poverty in the rural Third World. Central to the problem of agricultural development, and indeed to economic development in general is the rapid growth of the rural population. Until the beginning of this century famine and epidemics ensured that there were few periods of sustained population growth. Since the 1920s the rapid fall in mortality without any substantial reduction in fertility has led to rates of increase of between 2 and 3 per cent per annum throughout the Third World. In spite of the accelerating migration from the country to the town, rural populations have grown hugely. This has made farms even smaller, fields more dispersed, and in parts of Asia and Latin America, created a huge army of landless labourers; in both Java and India about one-third of the agricultural population is without land, and frequently without employment for more than a part of the year. Even though there are undoubtedly opportunities for absorbing some of this labour by the adoption of more labour-intensive methods, the solution to the problems of the rural Third World can only come from an accelerated rate of industrial growth which can absorb the rural unemployed and provide the new factors of production which can raise productivity in agriculture.

6
Reform of Agrarian Structures in the Third World

Keith Sutton

> . . . a land reform is a revolutionary step; it passes power, property, and status from one group in the community to another.
>
> (*J. K. Galbraith*)

There are few non-agricultural occupations in the countries of the Third World and populations are increasing. Land is the prime source of wealth. In most developing countries the maldistribution of land ownership allows the small number of great landowners to form the rich and ruling class. Table 2 illustrates this excessively skewed distribution of land ownership for several states in Latin America and North Africa. In some of these countries this juxtaposition of latifundia and minifundia has provided the impetus for subsequent agrarian reforms. Before land reform in Egypt a mere 6 per cent of landowners possessed two-thirds of Egypt's farmland, and the remaining third was shared between 2.5 million peasants. The greater the demand for land the higher its value and rents become. With such assured returns there is great incentive for scarce capital to be invested in land acquisition when it is much more urgently needed in the other sectors of the economy that await development.

Agricultural yields in most LDCs are low per units of area and labour. So far the post-war increase in food production has been due mainly, though decreasingly, to an expansion in the cultivated area. Henceforth, increased food production must come from raised yields. Despite some movement of labour from agriculture to industry, in the short term the objective should be not to release labourers but to avoid releasing them in view of the present rapid population growth. The labour-carrying capacity of agricultural land must be increased

Table 2   Land ownership distribution in Latin America and North Africa

	Year	Large multi-family size		Sub-family size	
		Number of farm units (%)	Area of agricultural land (%)	Number of farm units (%)	Area of agricultural land (%)
Argentina	1960	0·7	18·0	43·2	3·4
Brazil	1950	4·7	59·5	22·5	0·5
Colombia	1960	1·2	44·9	64·1	5·5
Chile	1955	6·9	81·2	36·9	0·3
Ecuador	1954	0·4	45·1	83·7	11·8
Nicaragua	1966	1·5	41·2	50·8	3·5
Guatemala	1966	0·1	40·8	88·4	14·3
Peru	1961	1·2	75·3	84·6	14·6
Costa Rica	1966	0·9	41·4	68·0	3·2
El Salvador	1966	0·4	37·7	91·4	21·8
Honduras	1966	0·4	27·5	67·5	12·4
Algeria	1951–2	4·0	38·5	70·0	18·5
”	1964–5	2·8	25·0	52·8	10·0
Morocco	1961–2	2·3	20·9	40·3	7·0
Tunisia	1961–2	4·2	40·0	40·8	6·1
Egypt	1950	1·3	47·3	94·0	33·0

Note: 1 A proportion of the large multi-family farms may be modern plantations; others are estates subdivided into smaller enterprises worked by tenants or sharecroppers. The rest fall in between with some entrepreneurial activity by the owner or his agent.

2 The data for Algeria 1964–5 only refers to the privately-owned land, the bulk of the colonial estates included in the 1951–2 statistics having been converted into *autogestion* units (see text).

Sources: D. Christodoulou, 'Agrarian Reform and Population Problems and Policies', *Land Reform, Land Settlement and Cooperatives* 1973(1), 8–18. A. Tiano, '*Le Maghreb entre les mythes*', Paris, 1967, p. 281.

in conjunction with its food production and thus technical innovations should be yield-increasing, not labour-saving. It follows that those work practices that result in labour under-utilisation should be changed.

Labour absorption capacity of land varies under different landholding systems. Data from India, Illinois in the United States, and Chile show that in the smallest farm groups there are 0.64, 29.0 and

0.44 hectares per worker respectively, and in the largest farm groups, 6.3, 88.0 and 6.7 hectares per worker. This and other evidence shows that a small-farm agriculture can absorb more labour than a large-farm agriculture. A counter-argument is that peasant proprietorship duplicates and under-utilises buildings and equipment, but Japan has demonstrated that technology can be adapted to fit small farms.

One path to the increase of labour-intensive agriculture is through the subdivision of land in large estates. All too often gross maldistribution of land characterises the developing country and there is scope for agrarian reform to break the pattern and give the labour force the opportunity and incentive to exert itself more. Agrarian reform to tackle the stumbling block of land holding and tenure patterns, is held by some to be the *sine qua non* of economic development, the precondition for increasing food production and enlarging employment opportunities.

There is a difference between land reform and agrarian reform. Land reform may well mean little more than land redistribution, but agrarian reforms in Algeria and Taiwan can be fitted into this integrated programme that aims at reorganising the institutional framework of agriculture in order to facilitate social and economic progress' (Jacoby, 1971). It includes the redistribution of land, adjustment of tenancy conditions, regulation of rents and wages, institution of farm-credit systems, cooperative organisation and agricultural education. A schematic framework has been presented by King to illustrate the breadth of measures involved. Two recent agrarian reforms in Algeria and Taiwan can be fitted into this schema to illustrate the similarities and divergencies of approach. (Table 3). Unfortunately the term 'agrarian reform' is often used rather loosely for any agricultural programme regardless of whether changes take place in the landholding or tenure status. Others would maintain that a precondition for meaningful agrarian reform is the fundamental redistribution of land holding and tenure systems.

Productivity of land and labour relate to the incentives and protection offered to farmers by the agrarian structure and this structure should be central to economic development planning. Outdated landholdings and marketing systems have degraded the peasant from a factor of production to a mere tool for land exploitation. This strengthens the case that mere land redistribution is inadequate. In Guatemala, for example, the United Fruit Company's partial disposal of plantation land to the peasants was

Table 3   The application of a schematic framework for agrarian reform in Algeria and Taiwan

---

Agrarian
Reform
{
  Land reform
  (Land tenure reform)
{
  Land redistribution (also
  including consolidation
  and collectivisation)

  Reform of tenancy

Reform of complementary institutions (including: credit, cooperatives, marketing, taxation, labour legislation, price supports, settlement schemes, extension services)

ALGERIA

Agrarian
Reform
1971–3
{
Land reform
{
Land redistribution
  – public land redistributed
  – absentee landowners' land
    redistributed
  – excess land from large land-
    owners redistributed
Reform of tenure
  – restricted to owner-occupiers
    organised within cooperatives

Reform of complementary institutions
  – 'settling-in' subsidies to beneficiaries
  – production cooperatives, various types
  – service cooperatives; 600 (i.e. one in each rural commune)
  – new villages; eventually 1000
  – peasants' union established

TAIWAN

Agrarian
Reform
1949–53
{
Land reform
{
Land redistribution
  – ex-Japanese land sold
  – absentee landowners' land
    redistributed
Reform of tenure
  – new tenancy laws
  – rents limited to 37.5 per cent of principal
    crop
  – Land-to-the-Tiller Act, to convert tenant
    farmers into owner-occupiers

Reform of complementary institutions
  – tenancy committees
  – loans from the Land Bank of Taiwan
  – land redemarcation project, i.e. land consolidation

Source: R. King, *Land Reform. The Italian Experience*, (London, 1973, p. 3)

largely a gesture, for the UFC continued to monopolise the fruit market. Agrarian reform must contain wider institutional and marketing reforms to parallel the basic land redistribution.

Both internal and external factors affecting man—land relationships have to be overcome to achieve agricultural development. Tradition and religion strengthen the defences of the existing social order, especially where ethnic and racial differences underline class differences. Peasant society is weakened by its own hierarchical structure, and an early task should be to strengthen the peasants' bargaining power. Naturally, the powerful large landowners profit from the *status quo* and strive to negate any agrarian reform.

Technical assistance through the World Bank and FAO has largely concentrated on agricultural resource development, on purely physical development, despite growing evidence of the vital importance of non-economic factors. International agencies remain reluctant to support aid programmes affecting the institutional structure but without socio-economic and structural reform programmes, technical assistance remains 'aid which the poor people in rich countries extend to the rich people in poor countries'. Aid, preferably multilateral, needs to be concentrated on countries tackling socio-economic and institutional problems in agriculture, in particular land redistribution.

Land Redistribution – the Critical Factor

Meaningful redistribution of land entails a parallel redistribution of wealth, income status, capacity for saving, and political influence. It provides incentives for increased agricultural production and labour inputs and strengthens the peasants' socio-economic position. Elements of social overturning are essential but long-term success requires subsequent evolutionary developments. One can distinguish between constitutional and revolutionary methods of redistributing land. Both require studies of existing land and tenancy rights, land-use patterns, population densities, employment and productivity, to establish criteria concerning the maximum property sizes possible, the size of new holdings, type of tenure, and scales for compensation.

Constitutional land reform programmes have been fairly successful in Japan, Taiwan, Egypt, Peru and Chile but elsewhere in Latin America and Asia, as in India and the Philippines, vested interests have limited and diverted the reforms. Taiwan's programme, 1949–53, proceeded in three stages: farm rents were limited to a maximum of 37.5 per cent of the principal crop; land acquired from Japanese nationals was sold; and the 1953 Land-to-the-Tiller Act allowed the government compulsorily to purchase and resell land from absentee landlords and to restrict private landholdings to three hectares of medium-grade padi field or its equivalent. Despite evasion, 377000 families benefited through revised leasehold contracts, 140000 bought public lands, and 195000 purchased land through the Land-to-the-Tiller programme, out of a 1947 Taiwanese population of 6.5 million. Other results were improved income distribution, increased agricultural productivity, and industrial stimulus through increased demand for fertilisers, insecticides and consumer goods. As well as the agricultural production index (1953 = 100) rising from 74 in 1949 to 144 in 1961, 42 per cent of the cash compensation paid to landlords was usefully invested in industry and commerce.

In Chile in 1955 a few large *hacienda* estates controlled 87 per cent of the farmland. Chile's upper class of 81 700 persons enjoyed 66 per cent of total agricultural income, the rest being shared by 574 200 agricultural workers. In 1962 the Corporation for Agrarian Reform (CORA) was created; 1967 legislation strengthened its objectives. An 80-hectare limit of irrigable land was set for any property, with escape clauses. From 1965 until late February 1970, 19163 families were involved, about 4000 per annum compared with a declared aim of 17000. By June 1970 approximately 2.5 million hectares had been expropriated and redistributed and early case studies of the production effects show increases especially in cereals, alfalfa and garden produce. Yields increased too, wheat by 37.9 per cent, maize by 25.2 per cent and potatoes by 65.2 per cent between 1964–5 and 1967–8.

Only limited success can be claimed for many constitutional land redistribution programmes. Large-scale programmes in India, including attempts at cooperative farming, suffered from evasion and pro-landlord bias. In Punjab and Uttar Pradesh many farming cooperatives degenerated either into family enterprises or associations of non-agriculturalists. Frustration among Indian peasants is leading towards the unconstitutional occupation of surplus land.

Diverse Revolutionary Approaches

Alternative revolutionary methods of initiating land redistribution emphasise increased production rather than the peasants' aspirations to land ownership. Consequently, a second stage of collectivisation follows any preliminary distribution of estate land. The human suffering accompanying the enforced collectivisation in the USSR has somewhat obscured the success in production and productivity terms. Between 1950 and 1964 inputs in Russian agriculture increased by one-third while output rose by 70 per cent. The major example of the revolutionary approach and probably the most successful in increasing production and employment per unit is that of China. An initial redistribution of land and draught animals confiscated from large landlords developed through cooperatives into People's Communes. These large multi-purpose units manage their own agricultural, industrial, commercial, cultural and military affairs, and provide a suitable institutional framework for technical innovations.

The model for the revolutionary approach is far from standardised. Recent changes in Cuba and Algeria have involved the expropriation of large, often foreign-owned plantations and farms. Cuba decided not to redistribute the plantations which formed 57 per cent of its agricultural area but preserved them as state-run units. Elsewhere a land ownership ceiling of 402 hectares was imposed and later reduced to 67 hectares. The same was true in Algeria where European settlers owned 27 per cent of the agricultural area and produced 50 per cent of the country's crops including 90 per cent of its wine. When independence was declared in 1962 many European farmers abandoned everything, so that by the autumn 60 per cent of the modern farms lacked owners. Crops and jobs were being lost on these vacant farms and so the local people occupied them, forming cooperative, self-managed units. This spontaneous movement, to salvage jobs and crops, became the government policy of *autogestion*, later involving the nationalisation of the remaining French estates. The autogestion sector differs from earlier colonial farming. Holdings are larger, cereal area has increased, rearing is less important, and yields and productivity are lower than those achieved by the modern and intensive European farms. Autogestion represents social progress by restoring dignity, responsibility and initiative to the Algerian *fellah*. By refraining from an immediate redistribution of expropriated land Cuba and Algeria hope to have prevented the emergence of a peasant middle class in the former plantation areas, a likely obstacle to further agrarian reform.

Effective land redistribution necessitates numerous supporting measures. Of these, tenancy reform is vital where 'tenancy at will' or share-cropping agreements leave the cultivator without security and with very little incentive. Onerous share-cropping tenure prevails over vast areas of Asia and Latin America. If a share-cropper works on a fifty–fifty basis, an investment of 100 rupees only yields him a profit if the total increase in output exceeds 200 rupees; quite a disincentive. Tenancy reform has been fairly successful in Sri Lanka but elsewhere, especially in Latin America, the laws remain un-implemented, often only resulting in eviction.

A more controversial issue is the potential of collective and cooperative farming. Western literature often equates 'collective' with communism and violence. Israel's success in collective farming was discounted because of the settlers' religious zeal. Yet the coexistence of capitalist and socialist agriculture should be as feasible as the mixed economy approach in industry.

Many of the cooperative experiments, especially in India, were abused by landlords, often themselves absentees, who contrived to obtain the government subsidies without actually assigning land to a common pool. More successful cooperative ventures include the Sudanese Gezira scheme and the recent developments in China where progress reflects the capacity of collective farming to mobilise labour, substituting it for capital. Cooperation helps to· overcome limited resources of skilled staff by more efficiently using trained extension workers. Moreover, the collective farm forms an institution linking agriculture to overall socio-economic development. Where traditions of collective life exist, as in the African tribal context, cooperative farming forms a more logical development process than the impo-sition of Western-type individual farm holdings.

Agrarian reform is limited without the support of programmes assisting and strengthening the basic land redistribution. In addition to infrastructural development and cooperatives for machinery and marketing, supporting measures should cover agricultural credit, taxation, and education. The inadequate credit situation in develop-ing countries is largely responsible for the vicious circle of poverty and debt. Credit rarely comes through the banks but through landlords, traders and usurers at exorbitant interest rates. There are the dangers of credit only helping large capitalist farmers and being dissipated on uneconomic micro-holdings.

More realistic land taxation strengthens agrarian reform by tackling the political power structure based on vested land owner-ship. When the Philippines failed to legislate a tax reform bill in the early 1950s the battle for land reform was lost because fair land taxes based on the potential yield of land weakens land speculation. Land values are forced down to reasonable levels giving the genuine cultivator an incentive to exceed the level of productivity assessed for his holding. Under-utilised *latifundia* and the owners' political power are threatened. Furthermore land taxes act as a kind of forced saving to provide development capital for related industries and infrastructure.

An educational revolution must parallel the social revolution represented by agrarian reform. 'Colonial-type' higher education is largely unsuitable for developing countries; broader-based down-to-earth educational systems are required, dedicated to agricultural progress and socio-economic advance. An intermediate education system is required as well as an intermediate technology. The primary schools established in every collective *ejido* after Mexico's revolution, and the Russian and Chinese literacy campaigns, are more appro-priate than Western-orientated yet largely unemployable graduates.

The coordination of complementary measures and basic land redistribution is illustrated by Algeria's current agrarian reform programme which was initiated in 1971 to cover the traditional agricultural sector which had remained unaffected by the earlier transformation of the colonial farms into autogestion estates. By mid 1976, 1 001 738 hectares of public and common land had been redistributed to 87 641 beneficiaries. Detailed limits were set on private owner-occupier landholdings with the excess to be expro-priated along with all land from absentee owners. A census of both landownership and potential recipients of land has been carried out. A variety of production cooperatives are being established, member-ship of which is compulsory for beneficiaries, optional for older-established peasant farmers. A higher level of 600 service cooper-atives will organise all types of agricultural unit throughout Algeria. This emphasis on a cooperative approach will require the creation of grouped settlements, and an ambitious 1000 new villages programme has been launched. A 'National Fund for the Agrarian Revolution' will provide credit through the various cooperatives. Local political vigilance is ensured through the commune assemblies as well as by the creation of peasants' unions to which only smallholders and landless peasants can belong.

Difficulties of Implementation

'It is the implementation not the formulation of land reform which poses the greater difficulty' (Jacoby, *Man and Land*, 1971). In countries like India most of the upper class own land, forming an influential anti-agrarian reform 'bloc' which dominates regional and rural institutions and fights a sustained rearguard action against the actual implementation of the reforms. This accounts also for the diverting and dilution of much land reform legislation in Latin America as the reform officials colluded with the upper strata in the villages. The administration of any agrarian reform must be raised to the national level. Adequate salaries are required, especially for field officers, to negate bribery. Government support should be given to peasant organisations to consolidate the agrarian reform.

A critical administrative question remains. Should the reform be carried out simultaneously on a country-wide scale, or piecemeal, a few districts at a time? The latter strategy, while not overstretching administrative resources, is risky as landowners in adjoining districts pursue policies of disinvestment, or sell excess land.

Agrarian reform was recently resisted and reversed in Tunisia where cooperatives were used to introduce modern techniques to a badly structured agriculture. In 1956 Tunisia's agriculture showed a threefold structure: 4000 European farms averaging 200 hectares; 5000 Tunisian farms averaging 80 hectares; and 450000 traditional holdings averaging only 7 hectares in size. From 1961 settlers' farms were purchased and organised into cooperatives which adjacent smallholders were encouraged to join. In 1964 all remaining European land was nationalised and reorganised into these *Unités Cooperatives de Production*. By mid-1968 the 1586078 hectares in cooperatives represented one-third of the arable land. Particular concentrations were in northern Tunisia in the upper and middle basins of the Merjerda River. Within the cooperatives modernisation was started through crop diversification and land use rationalisation. Afforestation and increased fruit tree cultivation were involved. Yields did not diminish, yet neither did they greatly increase.

By 1968 one-third of Tunisia's agricultural land still belonged to 3000 landowners practising extensive agriculture on fairly good land. Agrarian reform via cooperatives held great promise for this area as it was more underdeveloped than the colonial estates of the initial reform areas. Consequently in 1968–9 the government extended the cooperative system to all the remaining agricultural area but the combined strength of internal and external vested interests proved insurmountable. The attachment of peasants to their plots of land, especially in the Sahel and Cape Bon regions, exceeded expectations, and was coupled with the opposition of larger, often politically influential, landowners. In September 1969 President Bourguiba reversed his support for the cooperative policy and much of the cooperative land was repossessed by its former owners. Of the 161 000 hectares in the Beja region's cooperatives, 70 000 hectares have been reclaimed, two-thirds of them then being leased to sharecroppers. Many cooperative workers were left unemployed as the Tunisian agrarian reform foundered on a combination of peasant obstinacy and the opposition of landed interests.

When external pressure supports internal landed interests the prospects of reforms are slim. Land reform is now not as fashionable with international agencies as it was in the late 1950s. High-yielding cereal varieties have permitted a technocratic euphoria to divert attention from the need for institutional change in land ownership patterns. The 'miracle seeds' can greatly increase food production in the advanced, market-orientated sectors of agriculture, but the ultimate development objectives remain the widespread social and economic progress of mankind. Following the United States, other governments have increasingly ignored agrarian reform in development policies. The strength of internal political forces against agrarian reform appears to have diverted the approach of agencies such as the FAO towards taking the line of least resistance.

Inadequate defence of agrarian reform characterised the Mexican agrarian revolution of 1910–17, which accomplished large-scale land redistribution and eliminated the *latifundia* system. Collective *ejido* units controlled 48.7 per cent of the cultivable area and 46.5 per cent of the irrigated land, but complementary measures were neglected. Eventually landed interests monopolised other resources and produced a neo-latifundism in marketing, credit and trade. Japan, in contrast, successfully defended and furthered its land reform. Laws were rigidly implemented until rural exodus resulted in manpower shortages and the need for mechanisation. A 1962 reappraisal allowed cooperatives, partnerships, and companies to enlarge holdings and enterprises. This flexibility reflects the fact that 'land reform is a permanent feature of any dynamic economic system' and that it must be constantly reappraised to increase production and employment opportunities in agriculture.

7
Technology and the Third World

Howard Bowen-Jones

The word 'technology' as first used in seventeenth-century England meant the study of the useful arts. Today, and particularly in the context of development, its use is frequently limited to cover the physical methods of doing or making things, the *how* of production. Technology, however, is fundamentally much more than a tool or a physical process. It includes the cultural context of tools and processes. It is for this reason that during the whole of human history the transference of technologies has involved more than relocation of machinery and plant; it has involved complex and irregular diffusion of ideas and values. The study of such diffusion is complicated by independent origination of ideas and methods in different areas.

Until fairly recently in human history such transference as took place had two major characteristics. First, it involved materials and energy-forms which were ubiquitous in type. Second, diffusion proceeded slowly in association with folk movements which involved contact and mingling between communities which were not markedly dissimilar in material equipment, wealth and wants. Today, however, material cultural differences between communities have been radically changed, and nowhere is this shown more clearly than between the developed nations and the countries of the Third World. But the time-scale has also changed. Communication in the modern world is rapid, and every community is now exposed to the ideas, values and physical processes present everywhere else on earth. Machinery and plant can be transported and material production can be established anywhere in the world within months, weeks or days. Simultaneously, the information explosion which has affected the whole world to varying degrees has made many inhabitants of the LDCs aware of their material poverty, in comparison with the material affluence of other peoples, and has given them new desires.

One prevalent assumption is that relative poverty, the realisation of which is itself novel, is associated with 'primitive' technology, which is slow to change. It is easy and apparently logical to proceed to a further assumption that a transference of 'advanced' technology to a relatively poor society will bring growth, development and the satisfaction of newly acquired aspirations automatically. Experience in a number of Third World countries is proving that this is not so.

First it must be realised that between the poorer and the more affluent countries there is no simple, stark technological contrast. The oxcart, still to be found in, for example, Italy and Bavaria, reminds us of two simple facts which even the most casual observations will confirm. Reflection will show that regional variations in the use of machinery — the most obvious aspect of technology — within even the most affluent countries can be as striking as differences between countries. Further, most of these regional variations are fundamentally rooted in the rural/urban rather than the poor/rich, dichotomy. No country has technological homogeneity; regional differences in levels of technology, in *per capita* income and utilisation of energy, lead to regional differentiation. In England the regional differences in *per capita* income, *per capita* utilisation of energy or other indices show clearly enough that predominantly rural East Anglia is in many ways less technologically or economically advanced even than the depressed Special Areas. Functional differences between town and country such as those in Sweden, the United States, Nigeria or Colombia remain fundamentally important.

Even in the urban context, such as in central Hong Kong and Lantau Island, different technological needs and demands reflect distinct and varied situations. In central Hong Kong the provision of adequate living space on difficult terrain for the high density population has required utilisation of building technology and planning organisation totally different from those associated with the market and small business milieu of the majority of the population. But on Lantau, the traditional system of subsistence and urban aggregation of fishers, farmers and traders remains little disturbed by technological innovation.

Facets of Technology

Technology, even in its most limited sense, includes machinery for

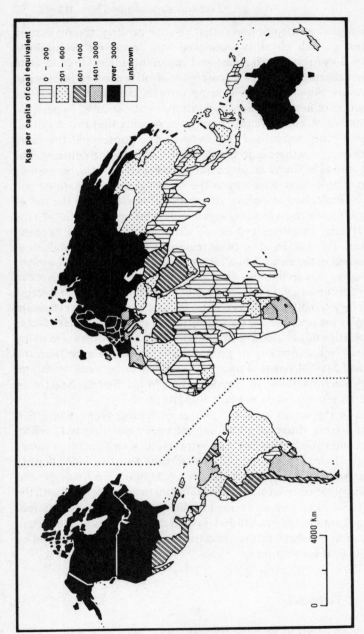

Figure 13 World *per capita* energy consumption (kg coal equivalent), 1970–2

kgs per capita of coal equivalent

0 – 200
201 – 600
601 – 1400
1401 – 3000
over 3000
unknown

4000 km

0

living as well as for production, housing, sewerage, communications, and many other elements. When life is functionally at its most complex, as it is in urban and industrial situations, so also are technological requirements most complicated. One of the great problems confronting the LDCs at the present time is, therefore, a consequence of the vast increase in urbanisation, much of which involves the acculturation of first generation townsfolk, many of whom find themselves transported from the simple functionalism of peasant villages to the delicate and complex machinery of city life. It is perhaps in the field of urban and settlement studies that cultural clash and technological anachronism need especially to be studied if urban growth in the LDCs is to be anything other than counter-productive.

We must recognise that simple, traditional types of technological transference still occur. In 1971 the Iraqi colonist could still bring, say to one of the Trucial States, the same technology of tillage which first spread from near his homeland 5000 or more years ago. For the most part however, the flood of factory industry products has left few lands untouched and it becomes difficult to distinguish indigenous technological creativity from mere opportunistic adaptation which, at worst, can result in the stifling of indigenous independent development. In southern Turkey, a tinker, who as a village craftsman plied his trade in completely traditional ways, used a discarded vehicle axle complete with differential gearing, two old bicycle wheels, some lengths of chain and scraps of leather, to construct an ingenious and effective animal-driven pump. Examples of this kind are readily observed in the developing countries and they raise the question: is this creative engineering or mere tinkering?

When we examine cases of the planned and deliberate introduction of new productive factors still at an apparently simple level, we recognise that the elements essential to the success of technological transfer fall under the heads 'motivation' and 'comprehension'. In Malta during the 1950s, the government decided on a policy which linked social welfare (through the expansion of milk consumption), medical welfare (the suppression of brucellosis carried in fresh goats' milk), and agricultural development (improved resource use and livestock profitability), and imported a large herd of first-quality Friesian cattle. These heifers in calf were distributed on an exchange basis to Maltese goat-herders, the assumption being that this would raise the technological standards of livestock farming. However, neither the motivation nor the capabilities of the goat-herders matched government policy. The recipients of the cattle could not, on the basis of their experience, comprehend that these heifers and their calves, as products of alien advanced animal breeding and nutrition technologies, were also delicate and sensitive organisms. Neither did their motivation, the production of milk with minimal feeding inputs, meet the actual requirements. The results were catastrophic and often visually vivid, as Friesian calves were seen hopelessly attempting to sustain themselves on prickly pear.

The transfer of technology, both in the form of equipment and consumption aspirations, is not solely to be associated with production. In West African and Asian bazaars and markets, imports of consumer goods which are the products of new technologies are strongly demanded by the populations (which increase even more quickly as other technological products such as water purification plants and prophylactic drugs reduce mortality rates). This can place sufficient strain on trade balances so as to encourage the establishment of import substitution industries. This cause is of course by no means the sole process leading to the transfer of manufacturing technology. But the relative ubiquity of relevant raw materials together with consumer demand has led to a considerable volume of rapid industrialisation in simple textiles and ceramics. Attractive to policy-makers, since such industries are relatively labour intensive and do not require large expenditures on imported capital goods or raw materials, developments such as these can often be successful because the technologies are intermediate between craft and science-based skills. For precisely the same reason, however, they may be more successful in meeting short-term commodity needs than in contributing to technological advance.

The more demanding technologies, potentially the more productive of dynamic growth, are the most difficult to establish because of the scarcity of skill and capital and the narrowness of the home market. When capital is amply available for the purchase of plant or expertise, quite remarkable technological innovations can appear. Kuwait possesses one of the most advanced hydroponics centres in the world, while the Saudi Arabian agricultural project at isolated Ain Haradh is technologically as advanced in design and as alien to its surroundings as is the desert electricity generating plant which maintains it in existence.

A further problem which faces developing countries is the adap-

Plate 1   In the Third World the need for education is paramount. In most developing countries 70–80 per cent of the population are illiterate. There is keenness to learn, as is shown in this village school in Nepal. (By courtesy, F.A.O.)

Plate 2   Degree ceremony at an African university. An indiscriminate adoption of the subjects, curricula, standards and styles of European universities may not provide the most appropriate education in developing countries. (D. Hilling)

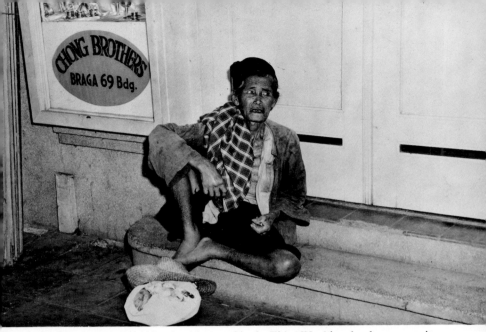

Plate 3   Malnutrition is widespread in the Third World and reduces capacity to work. This Indonesian beggar is suffering from beri-beri. His skin is cracked and his legs are swollen due to vitamin B and mineral deficiencies. (By courtesy, F.A.O.)

Plate 4   Energy is essential for agricultural improvement and industrialisation. An example of a simple wind-driven pump developed for irrigation in Ethiopia as a part of the 'Food from Wind' project. (Intermediate Technology Development Group)

Plate 5 A large New Guinea family in their home. Fertility is high in Third World countries and families large. Children can work and become an economic asset at an early age and are a support to their parents in old age. (M. J. Eden)

Plate 6 In an Indian family planning clinic a doctor explains the use of the loop to a group of women. Education in birth control is now important as a means of slowing down India's massive rate of population increase. (By courtesy, International Labour Office)

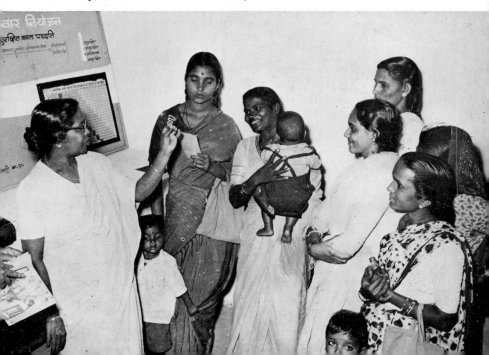

Plate 7   Hand-digging a drainage ditch in land newly reclaimed from the desert, Egypt. A plentiful supply of labour can be an asset, but the technology adopted must take this into account. (A. B. Mountjoy)

Plate 8   Nomadic and semi-nomadic ways of life are a response to the geography of semi-arid areas. These camel-owning nomads of North Kordofan, Sudan, are outside the mainstream of the country's economy and resist attempts to educate and settle them. (By courtesy, Ministry of Information and Culture, Sudan)

Plate 9   Two-thirds of the inhabitants of the Third World depend on agriculture for their livelihood. This scene of rice winnowing in Pakistan underlines the persistence of traditional and primitive techniques. (M. J. Eden)

Plate 10   Buffalo-cart, Pakistan. The use of dual-purpose animals – to give milk and to be used for draught purposes is common throughout much of the Third World. Fodder crops are rare and the animals, surviving on poor pastures, are generally of poor quality. (M. J. Eden)

Plate 11   Demonstration plots are an effective means of convincing farmers of the benefit of using fertiliser. Here in Java farmers from several villages gather to inspect the results of fertiliser application to different rice strains. (By courtesy, F.A.O)

Plate 12   In Ghana, government nurseries provide farmers with improved coconut palm seedlings to encourage production for a local copra oil mill. In this way industry and agriculture advance together. (D. Hilling)

Plate 13 Most agrarian reform measures include the establishment of co-operatives to assist the new small farm owners. At El-Harrinya, Egypt, an illiterate farmer is helped with the paperwork by co-operative officials. (John Topham/*The Geographical Magazine*)

Plate 14 The use of the right level of technology is all-important in introducing programmes of industrialisation. Western technology is expensive and usually labour-saving, whereas simple techniques may need less capital and offer more employment. In Sri Lanka an intermediate technology utilising bicycle wheels for spinning has been devised. (By courtesy, International Labour Office)

Plate 15   Intermediate technology can provide valuable work at the local level. Originally developed in Nigeria, the simple cassava grinder made from bicycle parts is now also being produced in Colombia. (Intermediate Technology Development Group)

Plate 16   'Head' loading, animals and bicycles still have an important role at the local level but such laterite roads, which corrugate in dry weather and may be impassable after heavy rain, will have to be improved for heavy transport. (D. Hilling)

Plate 17 Distance can be a critical impediment to the development of rural areas. Even a bicycle can greatly increase the range and capacity for moving gourds from field to market. (D. Hilling)

Plate 18 Early industries in developing countries supply basic needs for food, clothing and shelter. Small brickworks, like this one in Brazil, using local raw materials, rudimentary techniques and manual labour satisfy local demand. (J. P. Dickenson)

Plate 19 Simple labour-intensive industry, such as this Sudanese establishment making moulded concrete products, satisfies local demand and does not require great capital investment. (A. B. Mountjoy)

Plate 20 The Volta Redonda iron and steel works in Brazil, now the largest steel works in Latin America, was built during the Second World War with assistance from the United States. Such plants require much capital but often do not provide large numbers of jobs. (J. P. Dickenson)

Plate 21 Technical training is essential as industrialisation proceeds, for using expatriate technicians is expensive. Here student engineers in Cairo learn on the shop floor. (John Topham/*The Geographical Magazine*)

Plate 22　Shanty towns, or 'spontaneous' settlements, are now a feature of every Third World city. Squatters seize vacant lots and put up dwellings of whatever material is to hand – cardboard packing cases in this example from Khartoum. (A. B. Mountjoy)

Plate 23　Poorly constructed shanty 'in-filling' in urban areas provides not only homes but the workshop for a tailor and the shop front for the sale of local produce. (D. Hilling)

Plate 24   Another shanty example from Bangkok revealing the utmost poverty and the danger of disease from insanitary surroundings. (A. B. Mountjoy)

Plate 25   Singapore and Hong Kong are successfully tackling their squatter problems and hundreds of thousands have been rehoused at great expense in high-rise blocks. One such rehousing settlement in Singapore presents a gay appearance with laundry hanging from protruding poles. (A. B. Mountjoy)

tation of technology to the required scale of production. In order to match the small market for manufactures and heavy industrial products such as iron and steel, cement and fertilisers, a scaling down of the sophisticated plants is necessary, and this raises costs considerably. Estimates for one North African iron and steel plant were £18.25 per ton from a plant scaled down to produce 100 000 tons a year, but estimates were £15.25 per ton from a 1 million-ton-a-year plant. Agreement among a number of LDCs to establish one such full-scale plant between them would seem logical and economic, but the reality of nationalism makes this impossible to attain.

Intermediate Technology

Capital is generally scarce in the LDCs and this underlines the problem, for the technologies of the advanced countries are capital-intensive but labour-saving, and these conditions are directly opposite to those of most developing countries. The transference of such advanced technology consumes much of the developing world's scarce and expensive capital and offers relatively small employment in countries where under- and unemployment are acute problems. This situation and its implications became recognised during the 1960s, and with it the realisation that new technologies were needed. They have evolved as self-help techniques, technologies that could be afforded, that were easy to use and maintain and that would draw upon local skills and resources. These less sophisticated technologies suitable for small-scale operations come in between the traditional handcraft and the fully mechanised advanced technologies and have come to be called 'intermediate'. Intermediate technology is a more appropriate technology where labour is plentiful and capital scarce. In fact, given those conditions it may be the best technology, although as it is less prestigious and has an air of being second best it may have less attraction to certain planners. The movement to spread intermediate technology has advanced considerably in recent years, and is resulting in the introduction of simple, locally made ploughs and tools for working the land, equipment to grade and thresh groundnuts and corn, hand milling equipment, new devices for storing food and water, and the production of simple metal and woodworking industrial equipment. In India products of this type of technology include shoes, bicycles, electric light bulbs, and sewing machines.

In 1967 studies were initiated in Swaziland with the object of finding a tractor suitable for use by farmers. In 1969 it was decided to design and construct a prototype tractor at the Swaziland Agricultural College and University Centre. By the summer of 1972 considerable success had been achieved by combining local fabrication and standard imported components. What is important about this and similar projects is that transfer of technology is being combined with fundamental, indigenous technological creativity at a truly scientific level. It is the potential of this kind of dynamic, which characterised the flowering of the European Renaissance and the Industrial Revolution, that is now required by the less-developed countries.

This is the essence of the contribution which can be made to development by technological transfer. The importation of high technology is not enough if it remains alien magic. The bridging of the great gulf of technological incomprehension becomes a major development task in which transferred technology, of primary or organisational and conceptual type, has to be employed in order to make possible the productive transfer of other technologies. This is much more than a simple and uniform institutional and sociological problem, as we know from the varying speeds and success rates achieved in its solution.

The Maltese Minister of Education recently deplored the absence in her country of an adequate supply of trained personnel other than 'lawyers, doctors, architects, priests and administrators'. Exactly the same complaint was made in Malta a century earlier by the then Director of Education. The reasons for this static situation are attributed to the small population involved and to the long political history of dependence. But these factors, together with all those others which have given Malta a distinctive character, are so rooted in geographical complexities past and present that they cannot simply be eradicated by institutional change. A change of emphasis from general education to manpower training still requires an identification of training objectives. For many decades to come, differences in economic opportunity will continue to be determined in the LDCs by the material resource base, by location factors and by a host of interlocking environmental facts and forces.

In some situations the fear of underemployment may discourage some types of investment in capital-intensive technology, as in the communications industry of India. Also in India, however, in the

Punjab, the introduction of new crop technologies has recently encouraged both mechanisation and a demand for rural labour. Here, the successful transfer of appropriate technology can be shown to increase the total demand for labour and increase employment opportunities. The introduction of large-scale rice cultivation into the French Camargue during the 1950s was made commercially feasible by irrigation technology and the mechanisation of some production processes; this in turn vastly increased the demand for manual labour for transplantation, a demand met by Spanish contract workers.

There is no simple formula which may be applied in such cases. Changing or transferred technologies are always likely to produce frictional unemployment, the extent of which will vary with regional circumstances and potential. The only working rule is that innovation should give more room for development, should increase utilisable resource potential and should enable growth in other sectors. The transfer of technology remains most feasible when progress is slow but sure; great leaps forward are rarely successful.

Today, uncritical and uncomprehending technological emulation of the affluent societies by LDCs has to be accepted as a fact of life. The choice of the most suitable technologies is the main task of planning strategy but the success or otherwise of their attempted transference depends on an appreciation of geographical reality, ranging from spatial analysis to resource potential. It needs to be based on an understanding of the simple fact that any transference involves specific people in specific places.

8
The Infrastructure Gap

David Hilling

The term 'infrastructure' has come to mean all things to all people. It may be defined as comprising the basic services and public utilities essential to the commodity-producing sectors of an economy. A distinction is often made between the economic and the social components of infrastructure: the core of economic infrastructure comprises transport, communications, supply of power and water and social infrastructure includes housing and medical services. Education and financial institutions, a vital part of infrastructure, are not so easily categorised.

Broadly defined, infrastructure corresponds closely with what the economist calls 'social overhead capital' (SOC) and there is general agreement on the importance of such capital in the development process. Indeed, some economists would include as SOC everything that is invested before an economy 'takes off' into sustained growth. However, as there is no universally accepted general theory of the process of economic development it follows that there can be no agreement on the precise role of SOC.

At one time, the provision of infrastructure was the first priority, essential if investment in directly productive activity was to be attracted. More recently 'development by shortage' has been preferred: let the infrastructure lag and provide it only as pressure of demand requires. Japan, Turkey and Russia are cases where this approach has been effective. Hence infrastructure is not provided in isolation but as a part of integrated developing schemes. There is a danger, however, of creating one of the many vicious circles which bedevil life in the LDCs: infrastructure is not provided until there is a demand, but commodity-producing activity is not established until the necessary infrastructure is available.

All productive activities require some infrastructure before they can become operational. This either exists as surplus (be provided. Exploitation of natural resources oft investment, simply because the whole range of infra be created. The opening of iron ore mines in the w Kedia d'Idjil involved the construction of airstrips, 1____, _____, port facilities, two towns, hospitals, schools, commercial and recreational facilities, and the provision of water and electricity. This infrastructure was provided in response to a particular demand.

If, however, the infrastructure created in such a project is only just adequate to satisfy the particular demand, it is unable to attract 'footloose investment'. Such investments depend on a surplus infrastructure providing for reasonable anticipated growth in productive activity. Returns on capital invested in infrastructure are slow to accrue. Revenue-earning services such as railways, ports or power plants may in the long term be able to finance their own further development, but services such as education and medical care may be neglected, particularly as their impact on the development process may be less obvious and they may be viewed as the fruits and not as the seeds of economic growth.

Infrastructure and Qualities of Life

All the components of infrastructure are both the cause and the effect of economic advance, and the vast gulf separating the rich nations from the poor is reflected in the provision of infrastructure. Differences in the distribution of infrastructure give a basis for comparisons of the overall quality of life. The test of social achievement is not the annual increase in the output of society, but how well society addresses itself to improving the lives of its members. The infrastructure gap is startling and there is a clear and direct relationship between the average income levels and the range of non-monetary measures of infrastructure provision and the quality of life. With poverty is associated poor medical provision, high infant mortality rates, and a low expectation of life, poor educational facilities and high levels of illiteracy, low levels of energy consumption, and lack of communications and mobility.

Moreover, there is the tendency for inequalities within poor countries to be far more marked than in the case of the rich. Thus, whereas in the United Kingdom or the United States the top 10 per ent of the population accounts for approximately 30 per cent of the total income and the bottom 50 per cent for about 24 per cent, in the case of Mexico the top 10 per cent accounts for 42 per cent and the bottom 50 per cent for a mere 15 per cent of the total income. The LDCs are dual economies with small modern sectors which are often well provided for and usually in the urban areas, and large areas which are poverty stricken and have a traditional, usually rural-agricultural, economic base and totally inadequate infrastructure. In the case of Mexico it has been estimated that 40 per cent of the population has been almost totally excluded from the benefits of development. For many poor African countries the figure is higher. The economic development process is a complex interaction of numerous factors, no one of which is by itself able to trigger growth, but the emergence of a modern sector is primarily dependent on power and transport. For this reason the development plans of many countries have emphasised these two components.

Table 4   Population and Infrastructure (1975) (Percentage distribution)

	Popu-lation	Area	Energy consump-tion	Rail freight	Commer-cial vehicles	Tele-phones
North America	6·0	15·8	33·7	23·1	44·0	43·9
Europe	12·0	3·6	25·3	9·7	18·6	31·1
Oceania	0·5	6·3	1·3	0·6	2·3	1·9
USSR	6·4	16·5	17·6	54·0	6·9	4·6
Central & South America	8·2	15·2	2·4	1·2	4·6	2·4
Africa	10·1	22·3	2·0	1·8	3·4	1·2
Asia	56·9	20·3	17·8	9·6	20·2	15·1

(Based on United Nations Statistical Yearbook, 1976)

Per capita energy consumption provides one of the best overall guides to economic development. The contrasts are enormous and the relationship between wealth and energy consumption has provided the spur for many developing countries to embark on ambitious schemes to increase the availability of power. In Ghana the 768-MW Akosombo hydroelectric power scheme was heralded as the 'purposeful beginning of industrialisation' and now provides electricity for an aluminium smelter, a steel works, the bulk of the country's mining enterprises and an 880-km transmission grid which feeds most of the larger towns in the south of the country. Yet the domestic infrastructure gap has, if anything, been increased and, although total electricity consumption increased fivefold from 1965 to 1969, the north of the country has not benefited. Ghana is now an exporter of electricity to neighbouring Togo and Benin and in February 1978 contracts were signed for an additional hydroelectric power plant downstream from Aksosombo at Kpong.

Transport

Transport is one of the universal inputs in the development process and its influence is all-pervasive. A major United Nations report concluded that 'in most developing countries a lack of transport facilities is one of the main factors in world poverty and a major deterrent to rapid economic and social progress'. As a result of this lack of transport the exploitation of natural resources has been retarded, industrialisation limited, trade expansion and entry into the money economy hindered, and in all too many cases, including Zaïre, Malaysia, Indonesia and Colombia national unity itself has been put in severe jeopardy.

Purchasing power in the developing country depends to a large extent on revenue derived from exports, and exchange of surplus production and increasing regional specialisation are main features of economic progress from the subsistence level. Progress is also dependent on the diffusion of ideas and technology and it is clear that transport and communications provide the essential mobility of men, goods and ideas. Accessibility is, indeed, 'part and parcel of material progress', and the fact that transport plays a key role in development is one of the truths to emerge from economic history.

The mobility gap is startling. The world's main developed regions account for a mere 30 per cent of the world population, but for 88 per cent of the rail-borne traffic and 72 per cent of the world's lorries and buses. Although accounting for 37 per cent of the world land area, Africa and Latin America have only 7 per cent of the world's surfaced roads. If Asia is added, the total only rises to 23 per cent and it has been calculcated that if Africa, Latin America and Asia were to have a surfaced road density comparable with the EEC it would be necessary to construct nearly 32 million km of good roads. The gap is wide. It is clear that at one end of the scale are the highly mobile nations of the United States, Canada, Australia and some West European countries, while at the other there are countries such as Ethiopia, Chad, Indonesia and Iran which are highly immobile in terms of men and goods. Between 30 and 50 per cent of all World Bank loans are for transport projects, and a large proportion of planned investment in developing countries is in transport improvement.

The Changing Role of Railways

Many of the railways of Africa and Asia were built during the colonial era and military and strategic considerations were often dominant. Nevertheless many of these earlier lines did serve to stimulate economic development. Cocoa-growing spread rapidly in Ghana after the completion of the railways in the early part of the twentieth century, and in the six years after the arrival of the railway in northern Nigeria groundnut production increased fivefold. In Malaya, the expansion of tin mining and rubber production was greatly assisted by the development of the railways. In Brazil, coffee production responded rapidly to the provision of rail links to ports such as Santos.

The vast cost of providing a rail network, as distinct from a few separate lines and branches such as most LDCs possess, means that while the railways stimulated development in particular regions or at favoured nodes they have not generated widespread benefit and have served to concentrate the modern sector activities. Some of the newer railway extensions into western Uganda and northern Nigeria have made little obvious impact on the areas they cross, and it remains to be seen if the trans-Cameroon railway extension will be any more successful. It seems unlikely that the future will see any great increase in the railway mileage, and new construction is likely to be limited to cases where there are assured large tonnages of a bulk commodity. However, many of the new mineral lines are owned by mining companies and so intent are they on getting their ores to the coast that they are reluctant to take general traffic. Mineral lines may have little impact on the areas they serve and scarcely produce external economies for other sectors, as can be seen in Liberia.

The unlikelihood of railways producing general benefit means that roads assume the dominant role. Road works have the distinct advantage that they can be phased – in a primitive form they can be constructed by labour intensive methods, unskilled local labour and little capital outlay, particularly on imported equipment or material. They can be gradually upgraded as demand requires, whereas railways are very much an 'all or nothing' investment. Likewise, road haulage operations can initially be on a modest scale and have proved to be a most important area for local capital investment. The 'mammy' lorry of West Africa and its counterpart in other areas provides a flexible and economic form of transport for goods and people and is a major factor in breaking down local isolation and in extending the influence of the money economy.

The Stimulus of Roads

While never inevitable, the economic effects of road investment may be profound. Roads provide access to domestic markets and are an essential stimulus for agricultural improvement and expansion, a critical factor in areas where the population is predominantly rural and dependent on farming. New or better roads may result in changes in the distribution of population and certainly assist in providing rural populations with the social infrastructure they lack. By altering vehicle operating costs, better roads influence the quantity and nature of the goods carried, the competitiveness of exports and the price of imports. The establishment of industry will be easier and certain industries may be directly stimulated – quarrying, cement, tyre production, vehicle assembly and motor servicing and repairs (a valuable incubator of industrial skills). Roads may assist in forging national unity and may help to create the supranational regional groupings which some theorists think essential, especially in Africa where so many of the new states are extremely small. Countries such as Gambia and Gabon each with populations of 525000 provide minute markets and their economic salvation may depend on the emergence of larger regional groups.

Few countries would seem to be more aware of the possible advantages of road construction than Brazil, where a large population is markedly concentrated in peripheral areas and where large interior areas are sparsely populated and have a potential which provides a considerable challenge. The Superintendencia do Desensolvimento da Amazonia has been charged with initiating and directing development in the Amazon region, and while the area is well endowed with waterways, road construction seems favoured as the means of opening up the area and stimulating growth.

As part of the Brazilia project a 2123-km road was built in 1960 from Belem, the port on the lower Tocantins, to Brazilia itself and large areas of eastern Amazonia became accessible from the main centres of population further south. The area adjacent to the new route attracted population rapidly and an original 100000 has increased to 2 million and the number of settlements has risen from 10 to 120. Over 2000 km of feeder road have been constructed, agricultural production has been greatly expanded, the cattle population now amounts to over 5 million head, and a timber industry has been established. Traffic has increased so rapidly that the route, originally of improved dirt, is now being surfaced. While some question the overall environmental impact, so spectacular have been the results that the government has been emboldened to adopt a similar approach elsewhere.

In the mid 1960s a new road link between Cuiabá and Pórto Velho led to colonisation and also the expansion of tin mining in the Rondônia region. Pórto Velho has since been connected to Rio Branco and the Peruvian frontier and also with Manaos. In 1970 Manaos and Boa Vista, and Sao Luis and Belem were connected. The National Integration Programme of 1970 provided for a link from Cuiaba to Santarem and for the 3500-km Rodovia Transamazonia from the coast to Humaita in the far west. While these roads and their associated feeder routes are seen as the main means of opening up this vast area they are in fact part of an integrated programme which includes the improvement of river ports and navigation. The road construction provides valuable employment for Brazil's problem area in the north-east, but the main objective is agricultural colonisation. From the outset, the road construction camps are to be developed as the future nuclei and service centres from which the colonisation will proceed, and land in a 10-km strip either side of the routes is being allocated to farmers.

Africa too has its grand road projects. Following UDI in Rhodesia, it became necessary for Zambia to seek outlets to the sea through Tanzania, and the road to Dar es Salaam became the country's lifeline. This difficult route became known as the 'Hell Run', but has now been upgraded and surfaced and is a valuable international link. For the most part, road improvement in Africa has been piecemeal and the effect largely local.

In June 1971, at a meeting organised by the United Nations Economic Commission for Africa, a coordinating committee and a permanent bureau were created to supervise the construction of the Trans-African Highway from Mombasa to Lagos. A route was proposed and various alternatives were put forward by the countries concerned, mainly with a view to opening up their own areas of agricultural potential and to fit in with their own development plans. British consultants were commissioned to undertake a pre-feasibility study and a general route has now been agreed. The individual countries are now making arrangements for the construction of their sections of the road.

Although the total length of the highway will be 6393 km, for the most part it follows existing, albeit inadequate roads. Nearly one-third of the total is in fact surfaced already but parts will require design modifications to meet the standards specified for the new road: 1500 of the 2400 km of unimproved road are already included in the development programmes of particular governments.

The road will open up the areas through which it passes but this is not its prime function. Rather it is seen as a way of assisting the movement of goods from inland states to the ports and, more particularly, as a way of promoting intra-African trade. The road will link a number of growth areas — East Africa, Zaïre, southern parts of Central African Empire, Cameroon and Nigeria; it will have links with the proposed trans-Saharan and trans-West African routes; and the other feeders will in fact mean that much of tropical Africa is embraced by the new route system. It is also hoped that the road will stimulate the tourist industry on a grand scale.

While roads may well be the most important means of reducing the overall infrastructure gap, access and contact with remoter areas is often by air transport. In many LDCs the population is widely dispersed, distances are great, and the environment often hostile. In the mountain areas of the Andes, Himalayas, Ethiopia or New Guinea, in forest and desert, in the archipelagos of the Caribbean or Pacific, and where states are landlocked and far from the sea, the aeroplane is often the pioneer mode of transport. Much of the day-to-day freighting within Colombia is by air while in landlocked Chad in Africa the second most important export, frozen meat, has to be air freighted to coastal markets in Cameroon, Gabon and Zaïre.

The progress of the LDCs is largely dependent on their ability to export their produce, mainly primary commodities, and import the capital goods and equipment which is the basis of development. It follows that most of their trade is with more advanced economies – in the case of Africa a mere 6 per cent of the total trade is intra-continental and the rest is directed overseas. The ports therefore assume a critical role in development, and port improvement has been a main area of infrastructure investment. In West Africa port capacity·increased from 12 million tons a year in 1946 to over 220 million at the present time and deep-water ports have been built at ten places which were formerly dependent on primitive and inefficient surfboat and lighterage facilities. Continuing often severe congestion at ports such as Lagos, Lobito, Dar es Salaam and many Arabian Gulf ports also reflects the fact that in many LDCs port capacity is still far from adequate for their trade requirements.

In the LDCs there are large areas where human porterage and primitive forms of transport are dominant and where basic transport provision has still to be made. Yet this is a time of rapid and fundamental technological change in transport, and in Europe and North America freight is increasingly moved by highly sophisticated and extremely costly computerised container systems. It is very doubtful if such systems have any relevance for most of the LDCs at the present time, but it is certain that they are widening the infrastructure gap and making it more difficult for the LDC to catch up.

9
Industrialisation in the Third World

John P. Dickenson

It is often assumed that manufacturing is a recent element in the economic structure of the Third World. This overlooks long established craft traditions in many developing countries, such that they have been described as predeveloped rather than underdeveloped, having acquired significant technical skills before the coming of European colonial powers. Important technical innovations such as gunpowder, paper and clocks appear to have originated in the Orient, while Indian craft textiles found markets in eighteenth-century Britain. But as British manufacturers sought to expand, import duties closed that market and severely affected Indian production. Similar competition from domestic production against imports from the metropolitan powers led Portugal to ban the manufacture of all but the coarsest cloth in Brazil between 1785–1808. In the nineteenth century the intrusion of the colonial powers and the European Industrial Revolution had a profound and destructive effect on such Third World domestic industries.

Even so, the resurgence of manufacturing in at least some Third World countries took place over a century ago. In 1875 India had 19 cotton mills and by 1914 there were over 250, employing more than 250000 workers; other textile and metal working industries also emerged. Brazil's textile industry dates from the same period and by 1913 was producing 75 per cent of domestic needs in cotton cloth; a modern iron industry was established in 1888 and before 1914 chemical, clothing and food-processing industries had developed.

Despite these pioneer developments, Third World industry makes only a limited contribution to present world production, and to domestic product and employment. Less than one-fifth of the world's manufactured goods, and a still smaller proportion of its export manufactures and capital goods come from the Third World. Manufacturing provides less than 15 per cent of gross domestic product in African countries, 15–20 per cent in Asia and 15–30 per cent in Latin America. With the exception of Hong Kong, manufacturing generates less than one-third of employment in the Third World.

Colonial policies served to inhibit industrialisation and though political independence has afforded opportunities for development, progress has been comparatively slow in the face of various obstacles. The resource endowment in general is not an inhibiting factor, given the sustenance that Third World raw materials give to First World industries. Nevertheless, individual countries lack particular resources, and resource exploitation is often impeded by infrastructural deficiencies. More important are shortages of educated and skilled labour, and of physical and financial capital. The former may be obtained by education and training programmes and the latter sought from savings, export earnings and foreign investment and aid. Limited markets are a further problem. Given the poverty of the Third World, demand for manufactured goods is limited, and the problem is compounded by the fact that in many countries which are seeking to industrialise, their internal markets are not only poor, but also numerically small; more than 60 Third World countries have less than 5 million inhabitants.

In spite of these obstacles, and the economic arguments as to whether there should be priority in development for agriculture or industry, or a path of balanced growth, a recognition that manufacturing has some place in the economic mix of each country, varying with its resources and stage of development, has led Third World countries to encourage industrialisation. Given that the more developed countries are industrialised, industrialisation is seen as a way of generating higher living standards. It has been recognised that dependence on a limited range of primary exports poses uncertainties as to export earnings, a situation aggravated by rising prices for manufactured imports which have not been paralleled by rises in export commodity prices. Difficulties in obtaining manufactures during the Second World War were a further factor. It is also argued that industrialisation will help to absorb excess population unemployed or underemployed in the rural agricultural sector. As an extension of First World experience it is argued that industrialisation and urbanisation will lead to a fall in population growth rates.

Industry is also seen as being both more productive and more flexible than agriculture.

In those Third World countries which were industrial pioneers in the late nineteenth century, consumer industries were amongst the earliest to develop and provided food, clothing and shelter. Such industries expanded out of pre-existing craft traditions and began to utilise factory methods and imported machinery. Coffee production in the state of São Paulo in Brazil generated prosperity, 'know-how', infrastructure and a market, which resulted in the creation of textile mills and other industries. In 1895 the state had 11 factories with more than 100 workers — in textiles, hat manufacture, match making, iron founding and railway engineering. A similar pattern characterised the Antioquia region of Colombia, around Medellín. Clusters of raw materials, entrepreneurs and sufficiently large and prosperous local markets provided the base upon which industrial growth took place.

Over much of the Third World however this experience was the exception rather than the rule. In inter-tropical Africa there was little development of this type until recently. Early industries were expatriate, set up by colonial or other foreign powers to process or semi-process raw materials for metropolitan markets. They had limited relationships with their locales, for though they used local raw materials and unskilled labour, both markets and capital were foreign. They represented islands of advanced economic activity surrounded by traditional poverty. The oil refineries of the Middle East and metal smelters in Zambia and Chile bore limited relationships with the surrounding land and people, a situation somewhat modified by recent expropriation or nationalisation of such concerns in parts of the Third World.

For many Third World countries impetus to industrialise did not come until the late colonial and post-colonial periods. In tropical Africa the British Colonial Development and Welfare Act of 1945 and the French Fonds d'Investisements pour le Développement Économique et Social, initiated in 1947, provided some base for economic advance, though their main focus was on infrastructural provision and agricultural diversification rather than industrialisation. In the industrialisation of the newly independent nations there has been a growing degree of governmental participation in the economy. The replacement of imported manufactures by domestic production, the process of 'import substitution', has taken place with tariff barriers to protect infant industries and state encouragement of domestic industry. The state has taken on a role not simply of providing advice and incentives to industry but also of initiating industrial growth, a role heightened by the fact that only the government can assemble finance and expertise from overseas to implement complex industrial and related infrastructural projects.

In the light of Russian experience in the inter-war period, many Third World countries have sought to industrialise within the framework of declared national planning. India was a pioneer in this, through a series of five-year plans which have operated since 1951, and within which industry's share of planned investment has risen from 4 per cent to some 20 per cent. Industry was envisaged as the main growth sector, and as being capable of absorbing the growing population. Particularly in the Second Five-Year Plan, 1956–61, India gave special consideration to 'heavy' industry. The grounds for this priority were that India's enormous population was likely to sustain a considerable consumer industry, but that as it would be difficult to import the necessary basic manufactures for these industries they should be produced domestically. A mixed economy was created in which some sectors such as steel, heavy engineering, and shipbuilding were to be the sphere of the state; some were to be mixed, with state and private ownership; the remainder, mainly consumer industries, were to be left entirely to private enterprise. Development has been achieved by a powerful system of licensing new industrial enterprises, price and other controls, priority allocation of foreign exchange for necessary imports, and by planned growth in the public sector. Objectives of the licensing system, which regulated some 70 industries, included development within Plan priorities, encouragement of small industries, and reduction of regional disparities. Considerable growth has taken place but achievements were inhibited by failures in the accuracy and implementation of plans, problems deriving from the agricultural sector, and population growth in excess of predictions. An overall industrial growth rate of some 7 per cent a year has been achieved. Cement output rose from 3.8 million tons in 1953 to 16 million in 1975, and steel from 1.5 million to 7.8 million tons. Recent plans have given particular priority to those industries with important inputs for agriculture, so that for example output of nitrogenous fertilisers rose from 200000 tons of nitrogen in 1963–4 to 1.5 million in 1975–6.

In pre-revolutionary China the industrial sector was dominated by small units of production, largely concentrated in the Treaty Ports, and had a marked degree of foreign ownership. After 1949 the communist government sought to restore industry shattered by war and, from 1952, to transform the backward agrarian economy to that of a developed socialist state, through the mechanism of five-year plans. The focus, as in India, was on heavy industry and in the First Five-Year Plan, 1953–7, almost 90 per cent of industrial investment went to the basic sector. Although detailed data are difficult to obtain, it appears that by 1959 a substantial shift towards manufacturing had been achieved. In the late 1950s development was accelerated, using China's principal resource, abundant labour, in lieu of scarce capital, to achieve 'The Great Leap Forward'. Thus, a policy of 'walking on two legs', or the stimulation of both technologically advanced, capital-intensive and small-scale, labour-intensive industries, was followed. Existing heavy industrial centres were expanded and new ones created, but at the same time small dispersed units such as the 'backyard furnaces' were established. This experiment did not meet with full success because of friction between economic sectors, insufficient transport capacity, and the failure of agriculture to match industrial advance. Policy was therefore switched to one resembling India's in which industries related to agriculture such as fertilisers, tractors, and agricultural machinery production were encouraged. Despite the difficulties, considerable progress has been made, and in 1975 outputs of 29 million tons of steel and 3.3 million tons of nitrogenous fertiliser are recorded, and an important cotton textile export industry has emerged.

Other Third World countries have followed less rigorous patterns of planned development. In Brazil development planning, though important, has lacked the comprehensive nature and long-term perspectives of Indian and Chinese planning. The pattern of ownership has also differed, with state ownership being confined to individual firms rather than whole industries, and with a large private sector, in which foreign investment has played a larger role than in many Third World countries. Brazilian success has been substantial, and industry now contributes more to gross domestic product than agriculture, though it employs only 16 per cent of the labour force as against 40 per cent in agriculture. Ninety per cent of manufactured goods are domestically produced, including over 80 per cent of capital goods, and industrial exports are of rising importance.

Some countries have opted against the early development of basic industries, and concentrated upon consumer goods, particularly those using domestic raw materials. Nigeria has fostered growth in vegetable oil, cocoa, food and fibre processing, and development in more basic industry has been confined mainly to cement production. Other nations have sought to develop industries aimed at export rather than domestic markets. Hong Kong, Taiwan and South Korea have utilised labour, acquired skills and saved capital to produce for foreign markets, in some cases using imported raw materials. Textiles, clothing, wigs, toys and electrical goods are produced for markets in Europe, Japan and North America.

Since 1945 Third World countries have achieved industrial growth rates of over 7 per cent per year as against 5.6 per cent in the already industrialised countries. Change in economic structure and a greater degree of industrial self-sufficiency have been achieved, but in general industrialisation has not matched population growth and urbanisation, such that it has not fulfilled its envisaged labour-absorptive role. In Latin America the rate of growth in manufacturing between 1960 and 1968 was 6.9 per cent, while gross national product grew by 5.2 per cent, but in a majority of countries the rate of labour absorption by industry fell below the rate of growth of both the urban and the total population. Between 1960 and 1970 Latin America's urban population grew by 4.2 per cent per annum, but manufacturing employment by only 2.8 per cent. In consequence a significant proportion of the growing potentially active population is not being absorbed into the productive process, but is being by-passed by economic development. This is particularly true of the population moving from country to town. In the developing world levels of open unemployment in excess of 7 per cent are estimated, and in many major Third World cities unemployment levels are estimated to be in excess of 10 per cent. There is additional evidence that unemployment levels among young workers, that is, the additional labour force coming onto the market, are at least double the rate for the labour force overall.

The question of appropriate technology for Third World industrialisation remains under debate. It has been argued that the ability to borrow an existing technology from the advanced countries, as France and Germany did from Britain in the European Industrial Revolution, is a factor favourable to the developing countries. This assumes that the current advanced technology of the industrialised countries is appropriate to the mix of factors of production available in the Third World. But, techniques evolved in the industrialised world to utilise a scarce and expensive resource, labour, are not necessarily the most appropriate for developing countries where labour is abundant and capital scarce. None the less there has been a tendency for politicians and planners in the Third World to favour capital-intensive rather than labour-intensive techniques in their industrialisation programmes. This pattern of capital-intensive techniques is particularly marked in 'growth' industries such as metal working, vehicle and chemical production, but it is also apparent in more traditional industries. A proposal in 1963 for the modernisation and re-equipment of Brazil's cotton textile industry carried with it the implication of a 30 per cent reduction in the labour force. A case has been made for the development of small scale industries or the use of some form of 'intermediate technology' with higher labour absorptive capacities. In both India and China, small-scale industrial development has formed part of planning policy, and in China over 26000 such units have been established.

Further problems relate to market size and costs of production. Industries have been developed behind tariff walls giving high-cost products, and especially in situations of inadequate domestic demand, plants work well below maximum capacity. In the United States industrial plants generally work at over 85 per cent of capacity, but many Third World industries average 60–80 per cent of capacity or even lower.

Another feature of Third World Industrialisation has been a continuing tendency for spatial concentration. Despite a greater freedom from the locational influences exercised by coal, steam and iron ore in the first Industrial Revolution, the availability of electricity, new raw materials and alternative resource uses have not resulted in the dispersion of industrial activity. In Brazil over one-third of the industrial labour force works in Greater São Paulo, and over half in São Paulo, Rio de Janeiro and Belo Horizonte; half of Mexico's industrial employment is associated with Mexico City, and 60 per cent is to be found in nine centres in China.

Market forces tend to favour capital investment in those places where returns will be highest, and in planned economies it is easier to plan for large-scale investment in a few chosen centres. Such a strategy may well contribute the most rapid rate of growth of national product, but may in the long term create serious economic and social problems. The experience of 'depressed' areas in developed economies suggests that these problems of regional imbalance are not easily solved. Though the Third World countries are experiencing rapid urbanisation, substantial proportions of their population remain in rural areas. Alternative employment opportunities will be necessary for those people which the agricultural sector is incapable of absorbing, using techniques appropriate to the labour force and resource endowments of these areas. In the early phases of industrialisation dispersion provides an additional cost burden, but may serve to create counter attractions to the migrant foci of existing industrial centres. In some countries industrial estates have been used to encourage decentralisation, and to reduce costs of infrastructural provision of energy, water and transport by focusing it on single sites. In India over 100 such estates have been created and in Brazil a dozen, with labour forces up to 16000.

In addition to internal problems, the Third World countries seeking to industrialise face wider obstacles. The inadequacy of their own markets causes them to seek markets in the developed world, particularly for those products for which they have an actual or potential comparative advantage, such as cotton textiles, clothing, shoes, leather and food products. They have argued for a changing pattern of trade in manufactures, in which such goods would be exported in return for capital goods and other technologically advanced manufactured products from the developed countries. These aspirations, formulated through the UNCTAD conferences, have met with limited sympathy from the developed nations anxious to protect domestic industries and employment. Tariffs, quotas and other devices are used to limit exports of such Third World goods as powdered coffee, cotton textiles and shoes.

Other possibilities for fostering industrialisation may lie in the encouragement of 'export substitution' industries, by which the primary products currently exported by the Third World, largely without processing, are subjected to a degree of domestic processing and exported to developed world markets as semi-finished or finished goods. This does demand the availability of inputs such as adequate electric power, but a number of products, such as Caribbean bauxite and Bolivian tin, are being used in this way.

The widening of markets within the Third World, through some form of economic integration also presents additional opportunities for industrialisation. The creation of common markets and free trade areas would provide larger markets and permit economies of scale in manufacturing and a degree of complementarity in the industrial structure of member states. Checks on such schemes may be imposed by inadequate transport links between member states, while internal competition may damage pre-existing industries and some states may be favoured more than others. There is evidence that Kenya was a particular beneficiary of the East African Common Market. In the Central American Common Market the concept of 'integration industries' was introduced in an effort to secure a reasonably equitable distribution of manufacturing growth, while in the Latin American Free Trade Area differential status has been given to the less-developed countries to protect them from the competition of more developed industries in Argentina, Brazil and Mexico.

In those developing countries not hostile to foreign capital the rise of the multi-national corporation poses some cause for concern. The nature of such organisations raises questions as to whether corporate strategies relating to employment, raw material use and markets are in accord with national interests and aspirations. American investment in the Third World in all economic sectors accounts for 28 per cent of total US overseas investment, but provides almost half of total earnings.

The recent and growing concern for the global environment, deriving from rising pollution levels and presumed limits to growth, also has implications for the objectives of Third World industrialisation. It is conceivable that extreme 'eco doom' views might lead to obstacles being placed before Third World industrialisation, while imposition of global pollution controls could raise still further the high cost of development. One controversial suggestion relating to the two problems of pollution and the need to industrialise is that future development of polluting First World industries might take place in the less industrialised and less polluted Third World. This and other fundamental problems relating to industrialisation await further discussion between the industrialised and industrialising nations.

10
Urbanisation in the Third World

Alan B. Mountjoy

Urbanisation is an indication of modernisation, the sign of growth and economic progress. The whole world is moving towards a more urban existence and whereas the process is more nearly completed in the small number of rich industrialised countries, it is only in recent years that marked urbanisation has started to sweep over the less-developed countries. Increasing urbanisation is now occurring throughout the developing world, unfortunately, however, at a pace far in excess of economic advances, and the Third World is now undergoing a great urban crisis on a scale unknown to the advanced countries during their main period of urban growth. All over the developing world, but especially in Latin America and Africa, there has begun a flight from the land: a tidal wave of country folk who now threaten to overwhelm the struggling cities and possibly even to bring about their social and economic disintegration.

In the advanced countries alternative employment grew up during a period of change and increasing efficiency in agriculture. Urban mortality levels remained higher than those of the countryside and helped to damp down the gap between growing numbers of workers and work available. Mass transport, allowing cheap long-distance migration permitted millions to bypass the new industrial towns and cities and to seek a new life overseas. Thus although a vast movement from the land took place, it was spread over a greater period of time and was not focused solely on the towns. The flood to the towns currently sweeping through the Third World no longer bears any relationship to expanding urban economies and opportunities: under-employment in the village is being exchanged for unemployment in the towns.

Rates of Urban Growth

It is the astonishing speed of urbanisation in the Third World that is so startling. Substantial towns doubling and trebling their size in a decade has become an accepted pattern. Algiers, for example, grew from 300000 inhabitants in 1950 to 900000 in 1960. Now it is one of Africa's 'million' cities. Accra, Lima and Nairobi record equally massive increases while Teheran, Delhi and Porto Alegre more than doubled in that period. Here and there a boundary extension may account for some of the increase, but generally the story is one of unbridled and unplanned expansion. As statistics become available they confirm that it is the larger cities that expand at the faster rate whereas small towns, particularly in Africa, seem to have little attractive power and tend to stagnate. This is confirmed by data pertaining to the world's cities of a million people or more; they are increasing faster in size than smaller cities, and the largest of them — the super-cities of 5 million or more — are growing fastest of all. In the past 20 years the greatest increase in both numbers of 'million cities' and in their populations has been in lower latitudes, mainly in the Third World.

The rate of urban population increase in recent years for the world as a whole has been calculated at 3.2 per cent, but in the developing world this figure is over 5 per cent and the annual rate of growth for the larger cities is even higher: Lusaka, for example, grew at an annual rate of almost 12 per cent between 1963 and 1968: the population doubled within seven years. By 1980 it is expected that eighteen cities in Latin America will have passed the million mark and four of them — Buenos Aires, São Paulo, Rio de Janeiro and Bogota — will each have more than 5 million inhabitants. Calcutta, already notoriously overcrowded and with an estimated 600000 entirely homeless, is expected to more than double its population to reach 15 million by that year. Such growth rates are far in excess of rates of natural increase and mainly represent migration to the cities from the countryside.

Why is this happening on so great a scale? First, compared with our own experiences not only are all the development processes in the Third World being speeded up, but also they are spatially concentrated. Attempts to develop the economy by an enlargement of its industrial sector are checked by the poor level of infrastructure available. The basic requirements needed by industry such as

Million cities

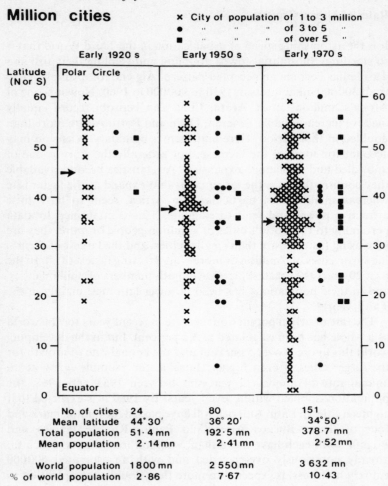

Figure 14   'Million cities' of the world in the 1920s, 1950s and 1970s

electricity, pure water supply, road, rail and port facilities, telephones, banking and insurance are to be found only in the largest of towns. Very often this is the capital, which may indeed be the only sizeable town and therefore assumes an exaggerated importance in the country. In such a town there is an immediate market for manufactures and an abundance of labour awaiting training. Early

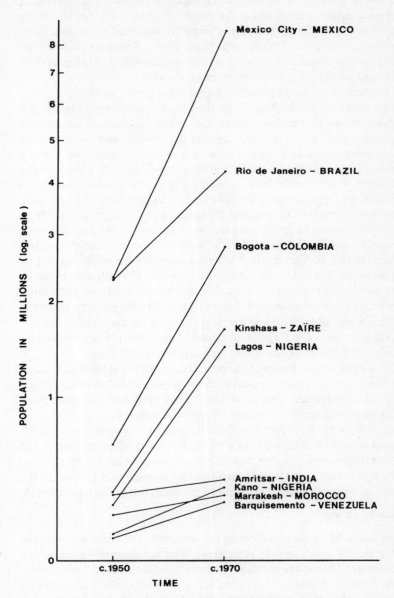

Figure 15   Growth rates for major and lesser cities

industrial growth has little choice of location and once established its presence enhances the attractive power of that town, for the more industries that congregate the cheaper it becomes to supply their infrastructure needs. Dakar, with 16 per cent of Senegal's population, accounts for 80 per cent of workers in manufacturing industry and 70 per cent of the country's commercial workers.

Second, in addition to what may be recognised as the 'pull' of a town, there is also a 'push' from the countryside. Opportunities for advancement in the rural areas are poor. Subsistence agriculture prevails over much of the developing world and methods of husbandry, hallowed by tradition, are generally primitive and, in Western eyes, inefficient. Agrarian overpopulation often leads to the farming of unsuitable land, to exhaustion of soil, and possibly to erosion and general land degradation. Fragmentation of holdings, too short periods of fallow, and the incidence of drought and pests all contribute to make farming a hazardous way of life. Where tribal rule prevails, as over much of Africa, land may be allotted or worked communally, neither method offering incentive for improvement or innovation. The extended family system which prevails over much of the developing world is a further disincentive to the individual seeking personal betterment, for his wealth, like his poverty, is shared with a multitude of kith and kin. It is against a background of chronic rural poverty, of a stagnating countryside, that the economic and social attractions of the towns may appear so alluring.

It is in the major towns of the poorer countries that the first signs of economic development appear with the growth of industries, utilities, services, amenities; and it is the towns that are foremost with education and health provision. A range of wage-earning jobs arises, especially with the expansion of the tertiary or service sector, even for those with little skill, making a higher standard of living than in the countryside seem possible. Social attractions become added to those of wage-earning, and novel amenities and amusements are part of the exciting possibilities this new way of life holds out to the countryman.

Shanty Towns

The outcome of the accelerating movement to the cities has been the accretion of great, usually peripheral, squatter areas of 'spontaneous settlement'. These are the shanty towns: the *favelas* of Rio de Janeiro, the *bustees* in India, the *gourbivilles* in Tunis, the *bidonvilles* in Algiers, the *ranchos* in Venezuela. Pathetic shelters built with whatever material is available: wood, flattened petrol tins, packing cases, straw, here and there decaying mud huts; little to ameliorate summer heat or winter cold. Cooking pots on fires in the open surrounded by pathetic rags of drying washing, rubbish and rats, open latrines and drains, the breeding grounds for flies and disease long-since controlled in the city proper. They are scenes of great poverty and discomfort.

Not all in these settlements are destitute: often chronic shortage of housing forces low wage workers to live there, hopefully awaiting better conditions.Others may have moved out of overcrowded tenement slums in the heart of the city to save paying rent and to start building their own homes under less crowded conditions. Given some security of tenure such squatters feel it worthwhile to improve their houses and by community self-help to install rudimentary services. Some squatter settlements occupy hillsides, as around Rio de Janerio and Lima: others have arisen amid marshy and malarial valleys as around Bahia, while in parts of south-east Asia such as Saigon, Bangkok and Hong Kong much of the squatter population lives on or over rivers, canals and lagoons.

There are, of course, variations in the pattern and character of squatter settlements. In Latin America and the Caribbean it seems that the shanty towns are rarely settling basins for new arrivals from the countryside. New arrivals go directly into the city, if only to be close to employment opportunities, and they populate the inner city tenement slums. From these slums they later move out as squatters to create illegal settlements. Thus by then they have urban experience and may have jobs; the move is generally to seek better conditions than in the slums. In time such shanty-dwellers, by communal self-help, tend to improve their dwellings and install basic amenities, particularly if encouraged by the authorities. Spontaneous settlements in Africa and Asia do not seem to fit into this category. Migrants move directly to them from the country, often to join others of the family or tribe. Density of population is often extremely high, poverty more acute.

Settlements of this character surround the major cities and continue to increase in size. Some sociologists regard them mainly as refuges to which earlier migrants and some urban-born population turn as part of their adjustment to city life, but a majority view is that they represent a halfway house between village and town – an extension of semi-village conditions where existence with relatives and friends is possible while the novel town life is sampled and casual labour sought. However, all too often the temporary sojourn becomes permanent as lack of employment blights hopes and aspirations. Thus the cell-like accretions to the city proper increase in size and present problems to the administration that are becoming insoluble. Immigration into Rio de Janeiro of the order of 5000 people a week is the kind of pattern that has to be grappled with by the largest of the Third World cities. Squatters make up almost 40 per cent of the population of Caracas, 30 per cent of the population of Djakarta, 45 per cent of the population of Lima, 50 per cent of the population of Ankara and 25 per cent of that of Casablanca. In the majority of cities in the Third World it is probable that the squatter element already accounts for at least 30 per cent of their populations.

Table 5   Uncontrolled settlements in selected developing countries

Country	City	Year	Uncontrolled settlement Total ('000s)	% city pop.
Tanzania	Dar es Salaam	1967	98	36
Senegal	Dakar	1969	150	30
W. Pakistan	Karachi	1964	752	33
Turkey	Ankara	1970	750	60
Colombia	Buenaventura	1964	88	80
Mexico	Mexico City	1966	1500	46
Peru	Lima	1969	1000	36
Venezuela	Maracaibo	1966	280	50

Source: UN General Assembly, *Housing, Building and Planning: Problems and Priorities in Human Settlements*, 1970

Some authorities attempt to distinguish between slum dwellers and squatters. Both live in slum environments but the city slum dweller pays rent and is a legitimate tenant. Tragically, slum rehabilitation programmes have lagged before the mounting pressure of the illegal slum dwellers, the squatters. The urban squatter rarely pays rent but occupies land illegally, putting up his temporary shelter wherever there is vacant land and ignoring urban standards of housing, hygiene and sanitation. In 1958 Lima had 100000 squatters, but by 1964 there were 400000, of whom 260000 were on land not designated for settlement under Lima's planning laws. Colonies of such squatters once established are difficult to evict and by now many have become organised sectors of urban society capable of negotiating with the authorities, their voice growing with the increase in their numbers.

The Squatter Problem

The flood of people to the larger towns in the Third World is now at a rate far in excess of the possible provision of jobs in those towns, and this rate of population accretion outpaces the provision of the utilities and services that are the hallmark of an urban community. To combat the squatter problem, in 1965 Brazil set up a National Housing Bank. This has become one of the most important social developement agencies in the country. Its prime tasks are to finance low-cost housing and to provide water and sanitation. Since 1965 it has provided money for over 750000 dwellings, but the *favelas* increase. Recently the President of the Bank pointed out that Brazil's cities would increase by 27 million inhabitants during the current decade, and that this represented a need for 5 million new homes and, annually, some 4 million water connections – this would be no light task for a developed wealthy country and it is doubtful if Brazil can accomplish it. In the case of Nigeria, it has been estimated that urban housing needs by 1985 will be about 200000 units per annum. The annual cost of providing this housing would be about £125 million, or a five- to seven-fold increase in current investment levels in housing. These targets are not likely to be met and the housing and slum problem is expected to deteriorate.

To some degree the whole movement may be regarded as an essential and even inevitable part of the modernisation of backward economies, but with it go serious and severe growing pains. Some field workers, especially in Latin America, accept this view and suggest that the shanty towns do play a dynamic role in the process of Third World urban growth. Stress is put on the fact that in city areas poverty is hopeful, whereas in rural areas it is hopeless. To the city migrant, particularly of Africa and south-east Asia, the shanty town is a reception area that has familiar overtones: it is not fully of the city, it has some resemblances to the village. Within it he may find tribal links and even relatives who can offer him help in achieving the personal metamorphosis that is to follow. Shanty towns become communities, leaders emerge and schemes of self-help may follow, such as in parts of Latin America, with voluntary work on community projects. With municipality help and cooperation, rudimentary streets, water supply and lighting may be possible on such a basis. What has to be recognised is that without such cooperation it is becoming physically impossible to provide the services of piped water supply, sewerage and sanitation, refuse collection, lighting, hospitals and education, and that it has become an impossible financial burden for the existing city dwellers to bear, for squatters pay no rates or taxes. The outcome is a worsening of slum conditions, for all too often helpless officialdom turns its back on the problems, seemingly oblivious to the tensions and forces being generated in the crowded, squatter colonies.

Despite the hopeful views of the Latin American sociologists, there is, in Africa and South-east Asia, a general view that over-rapid movement to towns and cities leads to a complexity of social ills. Overcrowding, lack of sanitation and disregard of hygiene frequently lead to sickness and disease. The *bidonvilles* of Tripoli suffered a typhus epidemic at the end of the war and later smallpox and tuberculosis became rife. The preponderance of young males among the newcomers distorts the population structure and leads to the problems of delinquency, waning moral standards, sexual infidelity, broken marriages, prostitution and veneral disease. A danger that at last is becoming recognised is the moral and physical breakdown of urban living patterns in the Third World; that is, patterns and style of urban living derived from the developed countries. Over-rapid urban growth has become a rash that could affect the whole urban body.

There are also political overtones. It is in the towns that much of the political life of the Third World is to be found: meetings, newspapers, and speakers can bring new ideas and stir opinions. A discontented urban proletariat can become a far more effective force for change than ten times its number of dissatisfied farmers; it is more easily swayed by demagogues and provides an uncertain but volatile element in the urban community. More serious, to the detriment of long-term national development plans, pressures may be exerted to channel more and more development capital to the short-term end of alleviating urban distress. Increasingly political decisions in the social and economic fields may be affected by discontented urban masses.

To clear away shanty towns and to provide cheap proper housing takes time and vast expense, but it might be possible if the flow of population into the large towns could be abated. To some extent, making the lesser towns economically more attractive might help, but the root cause that remedial measures should strike at is the considerable differential between economic opportunity in town and country. The growing power of trades unions in the large towns is becoming evident in their forcing up of urban wages. Government employees in the public sector are usually best organised and their wage increases act as a base for a wide pattern of urban wage increases. The economy of the rural sector is based substantially upon subsistence agriculture and the gap between rural and urban incomes grows wider. In 1968 the average Zambian small farmer was less than half as well off as the urban worker with whom he had been on a par in 1964. An inquiry in Uganda in 1966 revealed that the cash and kind income of the average farmer was £60 per annum, whereas the average unskilled urban worker earned £125 per annum. Annual incomes per urban worker are generally two to three times those of the agricultural worker: here is the core of the 'pull' the towns exert on country folk. One of the great resources that developing countries possess over the advanced countries is a supply of cheap labour, but if urban rates go on increasing and outpace increase of productivity, more and more capital-intensive processes will be introduced bringing in more and more labour-saving machinery: the result will be rising unemployment and a lowering of the general standard of living.

The relentless increase in urban population, far in excess of the town's absorptive capacities and their rate of economic development, indicates the danger of their physical, social and economic breakdown in the near future unless some remedial measures begin to operate. Rural development to reduce the 'pull' effects, to narrow the income gap between country and town, is urgently needed just as much as efforts to enlarge the productive employment structure of the towns. But rural development will become all the more difficult as the able-bodied increasingly leave the countryside for the towns. A Zambian minister recently stated that about 45 per cent of Zambians lived in urban areas, and of the remainder that lived in the country 70 per cent were old men, women and children, 15 per cent unemployable adolescents, and 10 per cent 'stay-at-home' idlers. Often policies of low agricultural prices favour urban dwellers at the expense of the farmer. All in all, it is not surprising that the able-bodied leave the land and flock to the towns. The present decade will be critical for many of the Third World cities. Unless these years are used to further vigorously measures to reduce the flow of migrants from the country, and to habilitate those already in shanty slums, then urban life in a number of these cities may well collapse. With limited resources available stark decisions will need to be taken if some control is to be exercised over the growth of the already bloated urban regions of the Third World.

11
Rural Development and Rural Change

David J. Siddle

A whole chapter of rural planning failures in Africa and the faltering progress of the Green Revolution in South-east Asia draw attention to the fact that in general the treatment of rural development problems in less-developed countries has been at best heavy handed and at worst grossly inept. While there are many contributory factors which are responsible for the failure of any single project there are three fundamental, interrelated sets of errors of approach which bedevil most attempts to create the appropriate circumstances for rural development. These are the errors associated with the demands made by governments for short-term political solutions to intrinsically long-term problems; the errors deriving from an overwhelmingly self-confident belief in the virtues of the Euro-American approach to development in which progress is equated with urbanisation and industrial growth; and the mistakes associated with a lack of knowledge concerning the patterns of life in rural areas.

The Short-term Solutions

Most first national development plans of new states were the product of political expediency. New electorates were deemed to need such symbols of independence as new airports, parliament buildings and presidential palaces. Such innovations were probably inevitable and possibly excusable as a means of achieving the immediate aim of creating some sense of independence and national identity. Less excusable has been the attempt to achieve results by similar methods in the field of economic development. Almost everywhere West European and North American models of growth through technological infusion, industrialisation and economies of scale have been applied with little regard to the real meaning of such changes for countries ill prepared for such sophisticated economic rationalisations. In terms of rural development we have seen and often still see attempts to increase agricultural output as rapidly as possible by introducing methods and approaches which closely follow Euro-American economic experience.

In some areas the 'commercial operation' is seen only in the form of the plantation and the ranch management unit, entirely given over to the task of serving the needs of a National Plan for rapid import substitution. Such large-scale enterprises are designed to create an impression in the annual balance sheet that the agricultural sector is vital, growing and energetically contributing to the export drive. Elsewhere it has been manifest in the form of a resettlement scheme run along project lines – a neatly gridded allocation of land parcels, specified services and prescribed and proscribed activities which appear crudely alien when contrasted with the tapestry of rural life which surrounds them. In Africa most of these schemes have been derived from experience of the similarly very expensive total failures during the colonial period.

Since the collapse of the Tanganyika Groundnut Scheme in the immediate post-war period there has been a proliferation of equally large-scale attempts to introduce West European concepts of planned development into tropical Africa. Resettlement and commercial farming programmes collectively costing more than £200 million have either failed conclusively or been only partially successful. The examples of disasters are numerous. The Gonja Village Resettlement programme was begun in 1950 and ended in 1956 after a total cost of £1 million. The Western Nigeria Agricultural Development Project began in 1948 and finished in 1954 after an investment of £500000. The Zandi Scheme in the Sudan operated during the same period and ended in riots and martial law, after a total investment cost of £1 million. Even the partial success of the Gezira Scheme in the Sudan must be set against the low level of investment in the rest of that country. In Niger, an elaborate irrigation programme was introduced in 1960 at a cost of 27500 CFA (Central Federation of Africa) francs per hectare with a yield to investment of only 6.5 per cent. A similar small-scale enterprise relying on local materials cost only 35000 CFA and produced much higher yields, yet even this scheme reduced local involvement to a minimum.

But this has not been merely a characteristic policy of colonial regimes. Independent African governments have been similarly tempted by such large-scale political and economic gestures. Major schemes of resettlement, irrigation, and power generation have involved major disruptions in the patterns of local life with, as yet, limited economic and social benefit to those directly involved in these disruptions. In all, more than 2 million people have been engaged in rehabilitation or improvement schemes of this kind, a population equivalent to that of several of the smaller states of Africa.

Such stereotypes of 'development' may provide short-term political answers by persuading an inexperienced electorate of the activity and dynamism of their new governments, but they rarely generate positive rural changes leading to a vital and essentially rural life-style. Nor do they provide for the needs of an individual already engaged in changing his economic base from the predominantly subsistent to partially commercial. Between the plantation and the settlement scheme, the ranch and the 2-hectare plot, the 'progressive' villager makes his accommodations to an increasingly complex reality. Impelled towards a positive identification of his status within a new political system and increasingly separated from his roots by the political and economic sophistication expected of him, he is obliged to find a new identity. The frequent spatial juxtaposition of so many approaches to agricultural production, which planning has brought to rural areas, and the encouragement to go in quite opposite and competing directions at the same time makes such a reality extremely confusing.

This variety of attempts to generate increased production is one of the most impressive and least studied aspects of rural geography in developing countries and it may be one of the most significant causes of rural decline. One of the harshest lessons of development planning in the Third World has been that rural development is not achieved by making such simple associations between input and output, costs and benefits. Piecemeal increases in agricultural services, improvements in the marketing infrastructure, rationalisations in farm holdings, and dramatic new settlement schemes, do not yield benefits which justify the energies expended on this type of 'modernisation'. It is now more generally appreciated that soil and weather conditions in the tropics cannot be treated as raw materials and that peasant farming behaviour is not controlled by the inflexible logic of West European economic theory. Yet in many areas the same pattern of mistakes continues to be made.

The recognition of the limited return so frequently achieved from large-scale investments has led not to a radical new approach but to the proliferation of alternative attempts to graft change on to a rural society by the induced diffusion of advanced technology. Development is still interpreted as the dissemination of the urban-based approach to progress, an impression which is reinforced in the minds of rural dwellers by the diffusion of urban manufactured goods and services and urban education, often infused along the communication lines of a colonial space-economy designed to abstract raw materials for export. The whole approach has so far been towards engineering a view of rural economic development along lines dictated by an external culture. There is a certain naïvety in providing a taste for the type of goods and services enjoyed by urban society within a rural environment and not expecting the inhabitants of those areas to migrate to enjoy these services and advantages in the urban milieu within which and for which they were designed. Explicitly rural services can only exist if they have a cultural base in rural society, otherwise they will merely be urban services extended, and inevitably less adequately extended, to the countryside.

'Agricultural' versus 'Rural' Development

Governments and agencies are at last beginning to learn the lessons of bitter experience: that there are few practical guidelines for realistic rural development planning in the Third World. The need for more realistic study of rural problems may now be apparent but it could be argued that there is little point in structuring better rural development models if real rural development has no part within the philosophical framework of development studies. The whole philosophy of 'modernisation' is still based on the concept of progress towards the good, that is urban, life through sustained economic growth. The classical view assumes urbanisation and industrialisation as both the *a priori* condition and the ultimate objective of modernising development. Seen from the office of the urban based planner the function of rural society, and its only function, is to produce a viable output to maintain the urban system upon which first Western cultures and now the urban systems of the developing world depend. In other words, the contribution of the rural majority

116   *David J. Siddle*

of the world's population to the civilising process has been an increased agricultural output, the main benefits of which accrue to the urban minority. Quite clearly it is *agricultural* and not *rural* development which urban systems require and most strategies of rural development reflect this assumption.

Given these basic tenets it is easy to see why 'rural development' has been interpreted in terms of 'getting the right input' (loan capital, expertise, technological aid, task training) and involves the assumption that rural society, to use an appropriate metaphor, is a static and even declining stock, best improved by new grafts rather than the application of fertiliser. Such a view is so close to being an essential article of faith that in most cases it is adopted with no further justification. This has had two related ramifications. As we have seen it has allowed the most violently disruptive interventions in the structure of rural society, justified in the name of rapid progress, and it has discouraged the examination of rural society as an entity in its own right.

Towards the Identification of Rural Systems

An increasingly sympathetic appreciation of the processes of rural change is necessary if there is to be clearer understanding of the impact of planned, urban-orientated modernisation on the structure of rural society and economy. This may now be the right time for such a reassessment. While it is still a major tenet of development philosophy that it is the metropolitan core which acts as the nub of the rural modernisation process, a growing lack of self-confidence concerning the merits of this approach to the attainment of the good life in Western culture has led to a more critical appraisal of its credentials as an exportable commodity to the rural developing world. Such a reappraisal opens the way to an examination of the whole conceptual framework of rural planning. Many social scientists, both marxist and capitalist, have worked hard to blur the distinction between the rural and the urban, pointing to similarities in class differentiation and economic motivation and the increasing number of linkages between those who live in towns and those who do not. The view of rural society and rural economy as a system of interdependent relationships, a distinctive sub-set within the urban system, is immediately suggestive of a more appropriate approach to processes of rural change. It reveals the pressures to which rural areas are subjected by their interaction with the metropolitan core and it exposes the intrinsically non-rural character of much development planning. It exposes the attitude of planners that it is not so much the development of the rural society but its incorporation within the metropolitan milieu that is needed. It can be argued that in most areas of the Third World rural systems which still have vigour can be defined and that preventing the erosion of that vigour depends on the clear theoretical and practical identification of the distinctive mechanisms of interaction between the social, psychological, spiritual, political, ecological, economic and demographic dimensions of a rural system. It is only by this method that we shall be able to isolate the forces which challenge the viability of such systems by concentrating attention on only one or two elements within them.

Rural systems rely on the balance of a set of values many of which are not 'productive' in the formal economic sense. In such a system agriculture plays an integral part, together with perhaps equally important elements like group acceptance, social interchange and inactive leisure. Agricultural activity, whilst it is certainly a necessary element, is not a *raison d'être* of the system as a whole. In following this approach there is need for a much greater understanding of the nature of perceptions and attitudes in rural society. We need to know whether these are modified through time in an evolutionary sense and how they are reacting to an apparently traumatic interposition of new values from another system. A systems approach opens the way towards more flexible evaluations. Not only does it assume a longer time scale but it also demands a view of processes which are rural; identifying the psychological, social and economic implications of the cyclic character of seasons and human life is equally important or more important than the linear notion of time which we are used to in urban society.

It will need the recognition that complex and subtle social, economic and ecological changes do in fact take place within the confines of apparently static and traditional rural economies. If a genuine attempt is made to bring non-disruptive change in the form of education, improved crop methods and intrinsically rural services, much more needs to be known about the long term evolutionary-adaptive changes that already manifest themselves but often go unnoticed. At the same time allowance for adjustments in a structure as a whole inevitably means a slower pace of innovation. For an understanding of such attitudes the logical cause and effect assumptions of Western science are not always appropriate. Just as Western medicine now turns with new respect to study the cures and medicaments of ostensibly more primitive societies, all social scientists would be wise to develop a similar humility in relation to alternative modes of thought. The close interrelationship between physical and human organisation between the seasons, animal migration rhythms and the organisation of clans and kinship in this way may be regarded as the subtleties of a balanced system and not always evidence of a primitive murkiness of thought.

The incorporation of these ecological checks and balances within a framework of a coherent cosmology which reveals a sound appreciation of the place of man in the local ecosystem is common to many peasant and pre-peasant cultures. The significance of other relationships need redefinition. For example, the relationship between kinship, house form, settlement structure and territoriality is a theme in a number of sociological writings. Study of the rural houses and rural settlement forms show that they represent a complex and highly structured view of the world which planning improvements may completely fracture. This research suggests that a number of serious problems of rural change may be attributed to the confusion and potentially damaging distinctions which geographers and some other social scientists make between social 'space' on the one hand and 'concrete' geographical space on the other. Such rural perceptions demand much closer attention from those engaged in planning rural changes.

Recent pleas for more research at the village level are a step in the right direction but the village provides only one level of focus for a study of rural development problems. The village does not exist in isolation. An individual settlement is one element within wider vertical and horizontal structures. Vertical structures may be defined by social and economic reciprocities and exchange mechanisms which find their most obvious manifestation, but by no means their only one, in the rural market system. Horizontal structures are revealed in the association of like settlements, linked by kinship and the associated evolutionary process of colonisation, which produces the pattern of settlement as a whole (Figure 16).

A positive approach to rural systems would immediately expose the inadequacies of piecemeal attacks on one or two areas within the system. Many avenues could be explored assessing the relationship

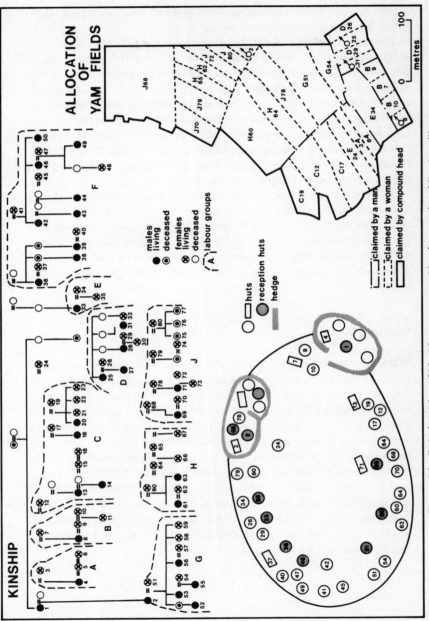

Figure 16   Relationships of kinship patterns and land tenure in a Nigerian village

between social networks, agricultural systems and marketing structures, but all of them depend on the adoption of new principles in examining the nature of rural change processes. There is a need for more emphasis on micro-scale studies refining the techniques of analysis on the research frontiers between geography, social and economic anthropology, and psychology. Currently tentative findings of research in space preferences, agricultural decision making, rural migration, the evolution of market and service infrastructures and rural settlement evolution may eventually provide a basic framework for the development of integrative models which are not based on the implicit assumption that 'development' cascades down the communication channels of the urban hierarchy.

This view of a distinctively rural society might be dismissed as a maudlin arcadianism in a new guise, representing a failure to recognise the harsh realities of urban migration, acculturation and population increase. But if the price to be paid for agricultural surpluses and urban migration is the loss, forever, of alternative approaches to the problems of the human condition, it may be too high.

Conclusion

While we must obviously continue to work towards the alleviation of physical distress, uncertainty concerning the long-term viability of our own economic and social system makes it possible to take a more sanguine view of the rural systems within which seven-tenths of the population of the world still operate. The 'long-term stationary equilibrium' or the 'low level equilibrium trap' within which many rural economic systems in the Third World are thought to be contained may require less patronising attention. Contained within some of their structures are complex adjustment mechanisms and sophisticated calculations of man-environment interaction, from which we could do well to learn. Radical new approaches in the social sciences are essential if the problems of 'rural' as opposed to 'agricultural' are to be faced.

12
Aid for Needy Nations

W. T. W. Morgan

We must embark on a bold new program for making the benefits of our scientific and industrial progress available for the improvement and growth of underdeveloped areas
(President H. S. Truman, January 20, 1949)

Aid has never been an unconditioned transfer of financial resources. Usually the conditions of aid are clearly and directly intended to serve the interests of the governments providing it.
(Teresa Hayter, *Aid as Imperialism*, Penguin, 1971)

If foreign aid were indispensable for emergence from poverty, the rich countries of today could not have developed because they did not receive foreign aid. . . .
(Peter Bauer, *Afrika Spectrum*, September 1967)

Most methods of raising the standard of living in the Third World require investment of money which, by definition, it does not have. International aid is a conscious effort to break this vicious circle with gifts and loans of unprecedented magnitude from the richer to the poorer nations. By 1977 the grand total of official aid had reached £8000 million a year, in addition to which commercial loans and grants from private agencies added approximately another £15000 million.

The potential of such an aid programme was demonstrated by the Marshall Plan in which the United States, with massive loans and grants, powerfully assisted the re-establishment of Europe after the devastation of the Second World War. In Point IV of his address to Congress in 1949, President Truman committed the United States to the wider task of assisting the poverty-stricken peoples of the world. The rapid recovery of the European nations enabled them to extend aid themselves and this example generated an enthusiasm for such international 'economic engineering' and in the excitement of decolonisation, national development plans were composed for all the newly independent countries and others.

A development plan contains a list of proposed capital projects which, working together, are intended to increase national output and the standard of living. It must also consider where the savings will come from to finance this investment. The low level of incomes in the Third World limits the amount which can be raised by taxation and this is largely swallowed up by the expense of maintaining the elementary services of government: administration, health, education and security. Profitable private enterprise will attract available local capital and, when this is inadequate, more can be borrowed from abroad at commercial rates.

Finance for public works is likely to be the most scarce. Roads, bridges and similar works do not provide a commercial return but form the infrastructure essential to the newly-established industries or commercial farmers. Hospitals and schools are welfare projects but they are also part of the modernisation of the country, increasing the efficiency as well as the immediate well-being of the people. Development plans therefore anticipate a supply of funds from abroad for public and private needs. In an analysis of eight such plans for African countries, between 27 and 51 per cent of the capital requirements were to be met from overseas. For most countries the foreign sources of capital are the developed countries of Western Europe, the United States, Japan, Canada and Australia who have formed themselves into the Development Assistance Committee (DAC) of the Organization for Economic Cooperation and Development. They are also the primary source of private capital (Table 6).

Table 6   Flow of financial resources to Developing Countries
(in US $million)

	1970	1976
Official Development Assistance	6790·5	13656·2
Other official flows	1138·7	3023·6
Private flows	6875·1	22185·7
Grants by voluntary agencies	857·5	1358·2
Total	15661·8	40223·7

Loans and Grants

International loans at commercial rates play an important part in economic development, and governments are rightly urged to encourage private and public overseas investment and to facilitate trade with export credits. What distinguishes the contemporary flow of capital from that of earlier times, however, is the extent to which it is composed not only of commercial transactions but also of grants and 'soft loans'. When derived from governments, either directly, bilaterally, or through international agencies, multilaterally, this is termed Official Development Assistance (ODA) which, together with grants from voluntary agencies, forms what would be generally recognised as 'aid'. The proportions of official aid channelled through multilateral agencies has been increasing slowly, and reached 24 per cent of ODA in 1975. This method of distribution generally prevents the tying of expenditure to any one country and diminishes the sense of political interference. It is therefore preferred by developing nations and recommended within the United Nations. It denies any trading or political advantage to the donor country, however, and this lessens the incentive to participate, while the arguments based on efficiency are double edged. A specialist agency can develop experience and expertise in the assessment of need and the application of aid which may be missing, especially in a small donor country. Some countries, however, feel that greater efficiency is obtained by direct control and exercise their own judgement.

The greater portion of aid is in the form of outright grants. Voluntary agencies range from *ad hoc* organisations, dealing with famine, earthquakes, floods and similar emergencies, to religious charities, Oxfam, War on Want, and others with long-established secretariats. As the volume of their gifts has increased, their activities have widened from spheres of social welfare to development projects, with the aim of securing a permanent improvement in the ability to maintain such services. Grants from governments similarly contain a welfare, as distinct from a development, intent but they also include the two distinct categories of food and technical assistance, in 1970 forming 14 and 47 per cent of the total. Particularly in the 1950s, food shortages appeared in many poorer countries and were met in a dramatic fashion by mammoth shipments of wheat from the United States, Canada and Australia. Beyond the basic need to save the starving and feed the hungry, food aid lessens the drain on foreign exchange and the amount sold provides local funds which can be used by the government to finance development or welfare projects. It has also enabled the richer countries to dispose of embarassing surpluses of agricultural production without offending rural voters at home. Food aid presents the paradox of a flow *from* the industrial nations, with a small employment in agriculture, *to* the nations with the great majority of the population dependent upon agriculture. Free imports of food can compete unfairly with local agriculture and so restrict the progress of the major component of the economy in developing countries. Fortunately the progress of the 'green revolution' is diminishing the need for food imports, and agricultural overproduction among richer nations is coming under control so that the importance of food aid is declining.

Technical assistance, the supply of teachers, technicians and advisers, remains of continuing importance, involving more than 30000 French and 7000 British teachers alone. This is attractive to the donor countries, in that salaries are paid to their own citizens, and beneficial to the recipients, because it meets an acute shortage of skilled manpower and enables the small number of local highly trained and educated people to be concentrated in the key positions in administration and armed forces where policy is decided and nationality is most relevant.

The presence of so many expatriates, often in conspicuous positions and enjoying high standards of living, can be a disturbing element and suggests a colonial relationship. Another politically embarassing problem is that the areas where such people are most usefully employed are often in their former colonies. This is brought about by language and other cultural inheritances in education and law. This is true of French, British, Belgian and Italian teachers who are working in Africa.

In addition to outright grants, loans are also considered as ODA provided they are 'soft' in terms of the repayment or the rate of interest they pay. Thus in 1970 the average length of such loans was 29.9 years, with a grace period of 7.4 years before the beginning of repayment, and an interest rate of 2.8 per cent. The extent to which this represents a gift can be calculated from the present commercial value of the loans, using a discount rate of 10 per cent. For 1970 this 'concessional element' corresponded to 57 per cent of the money lent. Much of this is lent through international organisations similar to the International Development Association which lends on soft terms –

0.75 per cent for fifty years – by contrast with its affiliate, the World Bank, which requires more commercial rates of return.

Sources and Amounts of Aid

The sources of the funds that have been quoted are the members of the DAC. Aid for the communist countries is less well documented, particularly the backflow, but is probably running at less than £200 million net per year to the non-communist countries, but substantially more to small developing communist countries such as Cuba, Mongolia, North Korea and North Vietnam. In 1975 Eastern Bloc aid to Indonesia totalled £65 million and that to Iraq £50 million. There is also a flow from the oil-exporting countries, mostly between Arab states. They transferred resources amounting to £5250 million in 1977. Of the DAC countries, by far the largest supplier of Official Development Assistance has been the United States, providing 32 per cent of the total in 1977. This reflects the role of America as the originator of the aid concept and its prominence in population and wealth. Ability to pay can be measured by the gross national product, and by this scale a number of other countries may be rated higher (Table 7). Thus the Netherlands and Sweden lead with 0.82 per cent of GNP devoted to aid, followed by Norway, France, Denmark and Belgium. Much of this money goes to current or former colonial territories and includes a large element of technical assistance – teachers and experts from the donor country.

Following representation of the World Council of Churches, by the United Nations Conference on Trade and Development (UNCTAD) and the Pearson Commission on International Development, the United Nations and the DAC have set a target for a transfer of 1 per cent of GNP to include both private and commercial loans and true aid in all its forms. Official aid should amount to 0.7 per cent. There is no objective basis for this target – it is not based on the amount which the developing nations could make good use of (investment capacity) or on the amount required to achieve any established aims of welfare, development or political stability. It provides a feasible goal and a stimulus to the less generous. It also supplies a more severe measure of the improvement in aid-giving over the years. Thus during the decade 1960–70, the value of aid from DAC countries increased by 45.9 per cent. Some of this was merely

Table 7 Aid contributions from DAC donor countries

	Total net aid at current prices (US $m)			Net aid as % of GNP	Net flow all resources as % of GNP	Grants by private voluntary agencies (US $m)
	1960	1970	1976	1976	1976	1976
Australia	59	203	385	0·42	0·57	37·2
Austria	n.a	19	39	0·10	0·92	11·0
Belgium	101	120	340	0·51	1·83	22·5
Canada	75	346	886	0·46	1·28	72·5
Denmark	5	59	214	0·56	1·27	5·6
France	823	951	2146	0·62	1·53	15·1
Germany (W)	223	599	1384	0·31	1·19	204·6
Italy	77	147	226	0·13	0·87	0·2
Japan	105	458	1105	0·20	0·72	16·2
Netherlands	35	196	720	0·82	1·96	30·4
New Zealand	n.a	22	53	0·43	0·48	5·5
Norway	5	37	218	0·71	1·51	19·1
Sweden	7	117	608	0·82	1·53	43·4
UK	407	447	835	0·38	0·99	47·0
USA	2702	3050	4334	0·25	0·72	789·0
Total	4665	6808	13656	0·33	0·97	1358·2

due to rising prices however: at constant values the increase was only 16.6 per cent. Between 1970 and 1976 the gross amount of aid doubled. However, the prosperity of the DAC nations increased so much that aid has actually diminished in relative terms, from 0.52 per cent (1960) to 0.31 per cent of GNP (1977). Much of this was due to changes in the flow from the United States which has diminshed in relative terms in recent years.

British aid effort has been consistently above average for the DAC nations although well below the United Nations recommendation. The British government has refused to enter a commitment to increase its international aid to 0.7 per cent of GNP although agreeing to a 1 per cent target to include public and private loans at commercial rates, and this is already operating. British aid per head of population, however, is well below that of many DAC countries (Table 8).

Table 8   Donor Countries' net Official Development Assistance per head, 1968—70 and 1976 (US $)

	Average 1968—70	1976
Australia	13·52	27·67
Austria	1·54	5·19
Belgium	9·15	34·63
Canada	10·53	38·24
Denmark	5·80	42·18
Finland	n.a.	10·78
France	17·06	40·55
Germany (W)	8·70	22·50
Italy	2·06	4·02
Japan	7·10	9·79
Netherlands	10·19	52·28
New Zealand	—	17·00
Norway	3·57	54·13
Sweden	6·68	73·97
Switzerland	2·48	17·64
United Kingdom	6·85	14·91
USA	14·81	20·14
Total	12·24	20·87

Source: OECD *Development Cooperation, 1977 Review.*

Unhappily the donor countries are few while the recipients are many and the volume of aid received varies widely between the different countries (figure 17). The largest single flow is to India, the most heavily populated of the poor nations, and similarly there are large grants to the great populations of Pakistan and Indonesia. The sums however are not proportionate to the size of the populations and the largest receipts per head are obtained by smaller nations. It seems as if donor countries prefer to attempt to make a significant impact upon a smaller economy than see their aid swallowed up tackling a vast and disheartening problem. Among countries with particularly large receipts per head are those of strategic significance, and some of the remaining colonial dependencies. Israel, Jordan, South Vietnam and Laos have received large sums from DAC countries while such countries as North Vietnam, Egypt (before 1976) and Cuba would appear to have been similarly favoured by communist countries. Remarkably large amounts of aid per head are received by certain small Territories such as the Netherlands Antilles

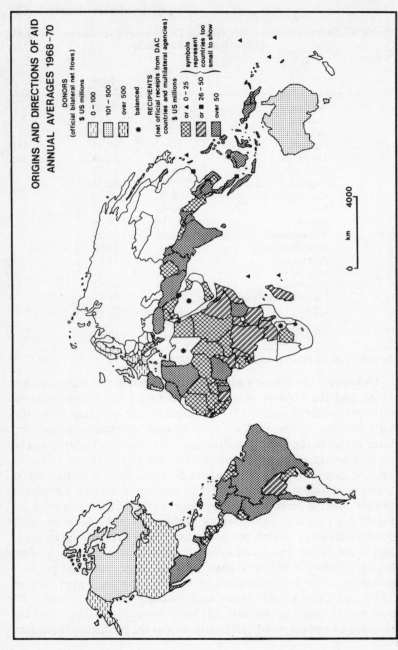

Figure 17 Origins and directions of aid, 1968–70 (annual averages)

and such British areas as Honduras, West Indies, Gibraltar and the Solomon Islands. Although Portugal raises a large amount of aid per head, the disparity of size with its overseas territories means that receipts per head are not outstanding. It is also noticeable that French aid is particularly directed towards her former colonies in the Franc Zone as is British aid within the former sterling area.

There is no widely agreed criterion of the volume of aid to be received comparable with the 0.7 per cent of GNP to be given. Instead, there are two concepts which tend to lead to opposite conclusions, one based on need and the other on effectiveness. A new British policy for aid announced in 1975 gave support to the former and aimed at concentrating help on the poorest countries, with emphasis upon increasing their agricultural production. The greatest human need is felt by those with the lowest standards of living, and here any aid is likely to be used for welfare projects and to increase consumption, with little permanent improvement. By contrast, aid to a less completely impoverished nation may effect a self-sustaining growth in productive capacity so that subsequent aid can be used elsewhere, and eventually the recipient may be able to become a donor itself. This dilemma was conspicuous at the third meeting of UNCTAD in Chile in 1972 when considerable differences of interest developed between a hard core of 25 of the poorest nations, mostly in Africa, and some prominent members of the Third World who are comparatively well-off: these were Brazil, Mexico, Singapore and Argentina.

Efficacy of Aid

Unfortunately it is very difficult to relate aid to improvements in economic performance in any conclusive or quantifiable way. Allegations of waste due to expenditure on prestige projects and corruption are common, and the administrative structure of the recipient government is unlikely to be very efficient. Some aid is deliberately intended for welfare rather than to increase output. On the other hand, the GNP in many poor countries is greatly affected by fluctuations in the world prices of the one or two raw materials, such as copper or coffee, which comprise the majority of their exports. Economic growth is obviously not merely a matter of priming the pump with sufficient investment. Painful social and political changes

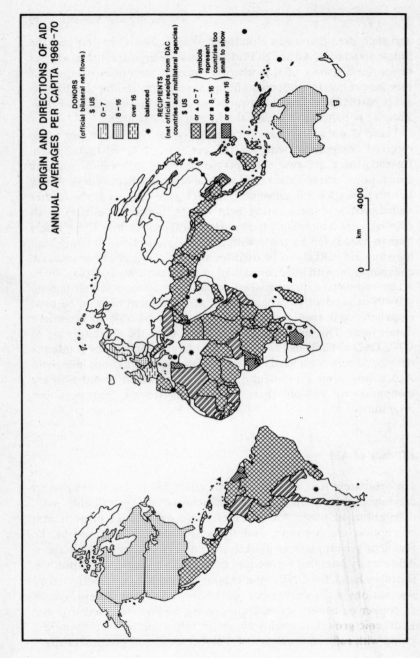

Figure 18 Origins and directions of aid, 1968–70 (*per capita* averages)

are generally necessary and these cannot be achieved easily or quickly. Nevertheless the evidence of the 1960–70 decade is that total real national product in the developing world is increasing and at a faster rate than in the developed world. Because of population growth, increase per head is less. Among countries with the fastest rate of growth are some which received a large amount of aid *per capita* in the past – Taiwan, South Korea, Ivory Coast, Thailand and Panama. This suggests that there is probably a critical amount of aid per head which is necessary for self-sustaining growth.

Criticism of international aid is widespread. This is not surprising considering the sensitivity of the donor/recipient relationship involving economic, political and social interaction between more than 100 countries. The value of aid may be limited by 'tying' purchases to supplies from the donor country, and waste may occur through inefficiency or corruption. The free supply of food can discourage the development of local agriculture and, similarly, facilitating imports of manufactured goods can hinder the establishment of local industry.

Two rather broadly based objections may be characterised as political interference and economic irrelevance. The disbursement of aid enables the donor countries to influence policy in recipient countries. Since the aid is being given to encourage development, activities on the part of the recipient that are considered by the donor country to be inimical, such as nationalisation without compensation or restrictions on private capital, might lead to its withdrawal. Undoubtedly such leverage is exercised and the opportunities for self-interested interpretation are obvious. Thus aid from the United States is not available, under the Hickenlooper Amendment, to countries which nationalise US-owned assets and fail to take steps to rectify the situation within six months; the extreme selectivity of aid from the USSR to states with a sympathetic ideology is similar.

On the economic plane, the supply of funds is not the crucial consideration in development but social and political changes are essential, as these could enable the mobilisation of local earnings and the emergence of entrepreneurial drive and a commercial framework. This will not necessarily be encouraged by an easy supply of foreign capital and expertise, especially as it will be channelled through government agencies. A *reductio ad absurdum* states that all economic contact between developed and developing nations works to the disadvantage of the latter. This flies in the face of the principle of comparative advantage, and the example of such countries is Burma. Since independence, Burmese policy has been to minimise external contacts, economic and otherwise, and the national income per head has stagnated.

Aid and Trade

A more widely held view is that aid would be better replaced by trade. A large and profitable volume of exports would encourage production within the developing country, provide the necessary foreign exchange, permit accumulation of capital from profits, and reward and encourage commercial innovation. The opportunity for political interference by trading partners is far less than that available for the providers of aid. In fact, much existing aid is intended to increase the volume of trade, and both public and private loans anticipate an expansion of exports, enabling the repayment of loans. To encourage this purposeful growth in trade by the Third World is the function of the periodic UNCTAD and its permanent secretariat. Protective tariffs have been a major hindrance because the poor countries are unable to offer reciprocal concessions which would compensate the rich for allowing imports which would compete with their own industries. Nevertheless a scheme for 'generalised preference' has been introduced and has lowered tariffs to the favour of poorer countries. This has been concerned largely with manufactured and processed goods on which tariff protection tends to be highest, with the exception of textiles. Textile industries are growing rapidly and are particularly suitable for the developing nations but the employment involved in these industries in the industrialised nations is so great that to remove protection would enrage a significant part of the electorate. Unfortunately, the United States has objected to such unreciprocated preferences as being against the aims of a universal lowering of tariffs through GATT. However, the result has been a welcome increase in the proportion of manufactured goods among Third World exports and encouragement has been given to local industry in the forms of indigenous firms and for international firms to establish branch factories.

The exports of many poor countries, however, still rely on a small number of primary commodities. Unstable prices for these on the world market discourage capital investment, forward planning, and the introduction of commercial cropping among subsistence peasants. Commodity schemes to diminish price fluctuations would therefore help in the process of development and their extension is favoured by the United Nations. Suggestions that such commodity schemes should be used to raise prices, however, face problems which were seen during the 1930s: new entrants to the market and consequent overproduction and price collapse. During the 1960–70 decade, export prices of raw materials and fuels declined but this was balanced by a small increase in the prices of foodstuffs and a 40 per cent increase in the prices for manufactures. The result was no change in trade terms.

The volume of trade between the developing and developed world is increasing at an accelerating rate although not as rapidly as that between the industrialised nations. This is encouraging since this is the direction in which the developing nations need to travel if they are to follow the previous experience of the developed nations. A group of more successful countries in this progression is emerging and may soon no longer require aid but will be able to offer it to former colleagues. It is this replacement of aid by trade which will measure the success of the present aid policies and enable aid to be concentrated in greater volume upon the very poorest cases.

13
Trade Growth for Development

David Hilling

All too frequently one is reminded of the continuing problem of the trading relations of the rich and poor nations. In 1974 a special session of the United Nations General Assembly was devoted to raw materials and development, the European Economic Community has created 'Stabex' for the stabilisation of export revenue for associated territories and successive meetings of UNCTAD testify to the lack of success in dealing with the commodity problem. If the oil price rises of 1973 and the apparent success of the Organisation of Oil Exporting Countries (OPEC) suggested a changing balance of economic power between the developed and less-developed it was soon to become clear that the changes were not as profound as some had hoped and others had feared. Recent violent fluctuations in the world prices of coffee, cocoa and copper dispel any idea that stability has been achieved for other commodities. The previous chapter has put some of the arguments for and against aid to the LDCs and also put forward the increasingly widely held view that aid would be better replaced by trade. Let us discuss further some of the implications of this view.

It is clear from the vast literature on economic development that there is no simple model to explain growth or retardation of growth. There is, however, a general recognition that for any area external trade is an important element in the development process. Much of the work on market systems has emphasised that at the local level the 'market place' is a vital interface not only for the exchange of goods but also for the personal contacts and communication of ideas which are the basis of the diffusion processes which generate change. The significance of this becomes apparent when it is remembered that the changing of ideas is every bit as important as the changing economy which is all too often overemphasised. What is true at the local level is also true at the national and international level – trade provides an important way of initiating and supporting change and makes it possible to exploit resources which may have limited or no value at the local level.

The classical theories of economics rest heavily on the concept of comparative advantage as a basis for exchange at all levels. It is argued that at an international level trade will lead to a division of labour based on specialisation and that this will result in equalisation of factor prices and incomes. In fact there is little evidence over any observable time scale that such equalisation does take place and many now argue that the outcome of exchange based simply on comparative advantage would be growing inequality between nations. As Myrdal has written, 'international trade and capital movements will generally tend to breed inequality and will do so the more strongly when substantial inequalities are already established'. The free play of market forces may result in another of those circular causations which seem to bedevil life for less-developed countries. The general arguments relating to the differential growth in 'centres' and 'peripheries' and the idea that 'backwash effects' from the growing points will hinder growth elsewhere are probably applicable at a world scale just as much as at the national or regional level.

The whole process of economic advance in the LDCs requires an inflow of capital goods and services that they themselves are unable to provide and which must therefore be 'bought out'. It is to pay for this increasing flow of imports that the income of the export base becomes essential. One might be forgiven for thinking that the LDCs live entirely on charity but in fact nothing could be further from the truth. In the case of all African countries, and that includes many of the world's poorest nations, 80 per cent of all their development is already financed by their own earnings from exports. Clearly they wish to bring this up to 100 per cent as quickly as possible but having achieved this, and the problems are legion, they may well be left with economies that are inherently weak. There is definite weakness in an economy in which foreign trade makes up a high percentage of the GNP and where domestic transactions are not considerably in excess of those effected externally. For real stability increased trade must also mean diversification and an associated growth of the internal market.

During the colonial era the superior and cheaper products of the developed nation were in competition with the product of domestic scale industry in the LDC. There was some export of capital to the

LDCs although the flow of development capital to tropical areas which now make up the bulk of the Third World was slight compared with that to other temperate areas. Such capital transfers were largely devoted to economic and social infrastructure or to the large scale production of primary products, mineral and agricultural, for export. There started to emerge the dual economies which are now character-istic of the LDCs, with limited modern sectors being far more closely tied to the developed countries supplying the capital than to the surrounding areas of traditional economic activity. The external orientation of such enterprises in terms of their capital, labour, skills and import and export requirements meant that 'spread effects' were often minimal.

The Dependence on Primary Products

However, colonialism probably strengthened rather than created the market forces which led to inequality and the overwhelming de-pendence on primary production in the overseas territories. Over 90 per cent of the export earnings of the LDCs is from primary products while nearly half of the countries concerned depend for 50 per cent or more of their income on one such product (see figure 19). It is therefore a combination of dependence on primary production and the limited range of such production which places the LDC in a vulnerable position both in that substitutes may be found for the goods on which they depend, and that the goods are often character-ised by demand elasticities which place them at a severe disadvantage. Thus, for a given increase in the standard of living in a developed country it is rare that a proportional increase in imports of primary products is required from the LDCs. Petroleum is an obvious exception and this accounts for its current influence on trading relations and gives to it a bargaining power unlikely to be possessed by many other primary products.

In the mid-1960s dissatisfaction with the low world price of cocoa led Ghana, then producing about one-third of the world total, to withhold supplies in the hope that the world price would then rise. The cost of providing storage for the large tonnages involved was certainly wasted money and the weak position of the LDC was amply demonstrated. Ghana's action had no impact on world prices, particularly as some of the richer nations, including, it was thought,

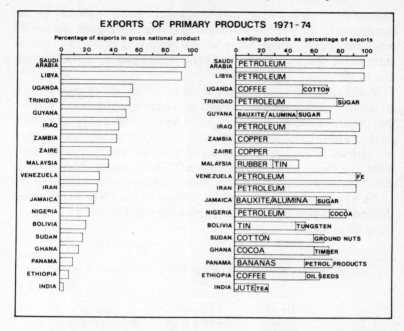

Figure 19   Exports of primary products for selected countries, 1971–4

the Soviet Union, leaked some of their cocoa stockpile on to the market. It was apparent that the LDC operating alone in this way stood no chance of influencing events but there was always the chance that if all the cocoa producers could act in unison then the potential was significantly greater. Such unified action is not easily obtained for the simple reason that given the demand characteristics for most primary products the export success of one producer is likely to be a lost opportunity for another.

With many of the Third World countries actively competing for limited world markets there is often no obvious community of interest to provide the binding force. The oil producers are in the happy position of being able to sell all they can produce. The world coffee market, despite the existence of the International Coffee Organisation, has over time displayed continuous competition and conflict between producers of the *Arabica* variety (for example Brazil) and those mainly African countries, whose output is of the *Robusta* type. There is also danger in the situation where one group of LDCs is successful in negotiating price increases which operate to the disadvantage of the other countries. The escalation of world petroleum prices, unless there are safeguards is likely to do more harm to the development prospects of non-oil producing LDCs than it is to the richer nations.

World commodity prices, particularly in the field of primary raw materials have always been subject to violent fluctuations. It follows that countries which are heavily dependent on a limited range of such products have considerable difficulty in making meaningful forward projections of income and hence in satisfactorily balancing their budgets. Thus, to take the case of Ghana again, there was a considerable accumulation of foreign exchange reserves during the 1950s when world cocoa prices were high. In the 1960s world prices slumped and rapidly expanding production did nothing to increase national revenue.

Table 9   Indices of World Cocoa Prices and Ghana's Import Costs

	Price of cocoa	Cost of imported food	Cost of imported textiles
1954	100	100	100
1963	36	126	131
1964	33	142	140
1965	25	161	175
1966	34	169	180
1967	48	174	188
1968	69	193	219

The low price of cocoa in the 1960s compared with the peak in 1954 had to be contrasted with the steady rise in the prices Ghana had to pay for all her imports. The terms of trade were moving sharply against her and the financial problems of the country in recent years, like that of many other LDCs, stem in large measure from such an adverse trading situation.

While these longer term price fluctuations make budgeting difficult, the average prices conceal violent short-term changes. Cocoa rose from £481 per ton in April 1973 to £500 on May 7th, £575 on May 16th, £640 on May 24th, dropped back to £545 on May 29th, and rose again to £590 on June 5th. Early in 1974 the price for a brief period topped £1000 a ton only to fall back again. Such fluctuations, the result of complex market forces, were repeated in 1977. Commodity trading is often highly speculative with vast paper transactions in 'futures' markets for mineral and agricultural commodities that are still in the ground. However, while such speculation is undoubtedly an important influence on prices in the short term it is certainly not at all clear whether it is to the advantage or disadvantage of the LDC in the long run. Some would argue that over time the average price is still quite closely related to the actual supply of the commodity and the real demand for it.

Price Stability and Commodity Agreements

It is clear that both the magnitude and the rapidity of changes in world commodity prices will have profound implications for revenue and balance of payments of individual countries. Since 1974 a fourfold increase in the price of crude oil has shown that price fluctuations give rise to changed flows of trade and foreign exchange and the need to consider seriously the recycling of such flows on the world scale. The benefits and burdens of such price increases are very arbitrary but without doubt the heaviest burden has fallen on less-developed economies such as India, Pakistan, Tanzania and Mali. The particularly marked impact of changes in oil prices has served to draw attention to, on the one hand, the advantages of coordinated action on the part of producers, and on the other, the need for much greater stability in world markets and prices so that the consequences of change are less arbitrary and disastrous. Over the years the LDCs have, not surprisingly, seen UNCTAD and the General Agreement on Trade and Tariffs (GATT) as a means of achieving the stability they seek. A number of commodity agreements have been negotiated and while they take various forms, in few cases can great success be claimed.

Price stabilisation is clearly in the interest of the LDC and has been attempted with commodities such as wheat, tin, sugar, coffee and olive oil. In the case of sugar, prices fixed under special international arrangements such as the Commonwealth Sugar Agreement may on occasion compare favourably with prices fetched by marginal sales on the open market but at other times may fall below. For the LDC such arrangements at least have the advantage of producing a predictable income over time.

In the cases of tea and coffee there have been attempts to regulate prices by limiting supply through the operation of a production quota for each producer. The fixing of quotas and prices invariably causes conflict and stress between the LDCs involved. The 1971 re-negotiation of the International Coffee Agreement led to a major dispute between Brazil, a relatively prosperous LDC, and a host of poorer African nations. Again in 1977 Brazil and Colombia combined to try to regulate the flow of coffee on to the world market and so maintain the price level but African producers were far from unanimous in supporting export cutbacks of this kind. There is a certain inflexibility in quota arrangements which are usually fixed on average production figures over a period of years. Thus the leading producers are determined to secure their share of the market and this must be at the expense of a country trying to break into the market for the first time or trying to increase its production. In the interest of diversification many LDCs want to develop new cash crops and may well find the quota system operating against them – another example of the LDC finding other LDCs rather than developed countries the stumbling block to its advance.

Another possible approach to the question of price stabilisation is that which has been adopted in the case of tin. An international authority has been established to create and maintain a buffer stock which can be used to influence market prices. At times of surplus the buffer stock is increased and is then let out during periods of higher demand.

In November 1974 the Council of Copper Exporting Countries (CIPEC) comprising Chile, Peru, Zaïre and Zambia met in Paris in an attempt to do for copper what OPEC had done for oil. Particularly they wanted to stem the declining price for copper which had fallen from a peak of £1400 a tonne in the summer of 1973 to £597. In February 1978 with the world copper price down to £620 per tonne, in real terms the lowest price for 20 years, Zambia, Zaïre and Peru decided to cut production by 15 per cent, a decision that did not gain support from the other members of CIPEC. However, the CIPEC countries account for only 50 per cent of the copper coming on to the declining market and other producers such as Canada, Australia, South Africa and Poland are not obvious associates in an attempt to control the market situation. Thus political cohesion has been very weak when compared with the oil producers: CIPEC provides a smaller part of the commodity entering trade than does OPEC, copper can be effectively recycled through the use of scrap thus reducing the power of the primary producer, and aluminium can be a substitute in some uses. Additionally, copper is largely consumed by three industries that are especially susceptible to the market — industrial machinery, vehicle manufacture and construction. It seems unlikely therefore that the copper producers will be able to reproduce the success of the oil producers. There does not seem to be much greater hope for the recently formed International Bauxite Association.

One reason for the general lack of success in creating producer solidarity is that the bargaining position is often very weak. In contrast with the bargaining strength of the oil producers, other mineral producers use more labour-intensive methods and restriction of output creates unacceptable social problems. Further, they are often in competition with the more advanced economies many of which have a range of mineral resources. Perhaps the conservation lobby will be more influential in helping the LDC sell its minerals by placing restrictions on development in advanced economies. The supply of plantation crops such as rubber, cotton and edible oils is not easily controlled in the short term, there is always the need to sell as much as possible at prevailing prices and there is frequently competition from temperate zone substitutes and synthetics. Temperate foodstuffs, jealously protected for a variety of strategic and social reasons, create problems of access for a range of tropical crops.

With the problems of obtaining international agreements in complex market situations some see greater benefit in medium or long term bilateral trading agreements. It is of course possible to build some price flexibility into such agreements but there is always the possibility that open market prices will move ahead of the contract prices. The ability of the producer to renegotiate prices will depend to a large extent on the demand for the product and the nature of the competitive forces.

While commodity agreements have in cases produced a measure of stability there has been general disillusionment in the LDCs on the ability of UNCTAD to provide solutions. The UNCTAD Conference of 1977 at which it was hoped to create a Common Fund for the stablisation of prices for eighteen major commodities eventually came to an impasse with the developed nations generally unable to tailor the Fund to the demands of the LDCs. Perhaps the most satisfactory, if limited, arrangement to date has been that negotiated between the EEC and its overseas associates. The idea of Stabex is that for a range of twelve primary products the LDCs are able to claim compensation if their earnings drop below certain agreed levels. A number of African, Caribbean and Pacific countries have already benefited.

Restrictive Trade Policies

It is now generally recognised that a main impediment to the trade expansion of the LDCs is to be found in the restrictive trade policies of the richer nations. The Pearson Report of 1969 recommended that advanced economies should be opened up to an increasing range of commodities from the LDCs and that their protective markets should give readier access to goods of all kinds. The EEC's Common Agricultural Policy is a clear example of such protection in operation and European policy is affecting LDCs in a variety of commodities — grain, beef, fruit and vegetables, vegetable oils, oilseed cakes and sugar. And for some but not all LDCs there are the limited advantages of being 'Associates' of the Community. Britain's problems in negotiating for sugar purchases from Guyana to meet shortages in 1974 illustrated some of the conflicts inherent in open market as against protective market arrangements.

In a number of areas UNCTAD has been successful in negotiating the extension by industrialised countries of generalised preference schemes for imports from LDCs. As yet these have hardly started to influence agricultural products but there has been welcome progress in the case of some manufactured goods in spite of numerous exclusions, escape clauses and tariff quotas to protect particularly sensitive industries. During the 1960s the LDC share of world trade in manufactured goods increased from 5.5 to 6.5 per cent, a small relative increase, but still faster growth than was recorded for trade in primary products. The success of the LDCs has been most marked in cases such as textiles, footware and leather industries where they can capitalise on their lower labour costs and compete effectively with labour-intensive industries in developed countries. Thus India and Egypt have developed considerable textile industries and are exporters in spite of the fact that industrialised countries have been reluctant to remove protection from such goods. The LDCs have also been reasonably successful in light manufactures (for example toys from Hong Kong) which are cheap to produce and for which unit cost of transport is low and are beginning to have some impact in assembly line products where labour inputs are high but relatively unskilled.

In recent years aid in its various forms has become increasingly suspect and it can be demonstrated that some aid has done little to advance economic progress and has possibly in cases even retarded growth. It does not follow that aid should be dismissed as generally unnecessary as a stimulant to economic development but rather that it should be applied in a more rational and selective manner. Of greater importance is that it should be realised that a rather more open policy by advanced economies with respect to trade would probably cost them far less in the long run than the aid they now distribute, and such a policy would certainly be of greater benefit to the LDC. Thus Europe pays heavily to protect its sugar-beet producers and then gives aid to LDCs which might need less if only they could sell their sugar in larger quantities!

While the trade of the LDCs has certainly been expanding in recent years, the growth rate is still well behind that of the industrialised countries. Further, it now claimed in many LDCs that the full benefits of this increased trade do not accrue to them since for the most part it is carried in ships belonging to the richer nations. It is not without reason that announcements of Britain's normally gloomy trade figures end by noting that things would have been a lot worse had it not been for invisible earnings. But such gain is somebody's loss and the LDC is concerned to conserve its hard won foreign exchange earnings. For this reason there was great emphasis at the Santiago UNCTAD conference on increased assistance for the LDCs in developing their own shipping lines. While the LDCs account for about two-thirds of the tonnage of world trade they control only 7.5 per cent of the world's shipping and they are eager to get into the shipping business in spite of its highly capital-intensive character and not altogether certain returns. Many of the LDCs have now established their own shipping companies (for example, Pakistan, Nigeria, Ghana) either operating independently or within the established framework of liner shipping conferences. While still not fully ratified, an UNCTAD convention has proposed that 80 per cent of the trade between any two nations should be carried, 40 per cent each, by the ships of those nations and only 20 per cent should be available for carriage by other parties. It is hoped by this to ensure that the LDCs participate more fully in the movement of their own trade, influence the freight rate structures, achieve a greater measure of bargaining power and improve their balance of payments. In this as in other attempts to improve the trading position of the LDCs progress will be all too slow and frustrated by the existing balance of world economic power.

14
Summary and Conclusions

B. W. Hodder

What can one say or do about the Third World after more than two decades of conscious efforts to bring about improvements in levels of living in these countries? Certainly one cannot point to any marked general success: rather there is a picture of confusion and disappointment. Absolute levels of income within Third World countries are often extremely low and their rates of growth are commonly slow or negligible. This means that by whatever criteria one cares to use, the gap between rich and poor nations is widening. The political and humanitarian implications of this widening gap are quite unacceptable.

However, the differences in levels of development and in achievement between the less-developed countries themselves are now becoming increasingly apparent. Several countries, such as Iran, Singapore and Venezuela, can now hardly be termed 'less developed'; and rates of growth in Korea, Taiwan, Ecuador, Malaysia and Brazil put such countries into a different category from those which remain extremely poor, like Mali, or which have low or negative rates of growth, like Burma, Mauritania or Bangladesh. At least in material terms, the gap between the poorer and richer less-developed countries is becoming as significant as is the gap between the developed countries and the Third World.

This fact has recently been highlighted dramatically by the sharp rises in oil prices. The oil-rich countries of the Third World have gained enormously: Nigeria's ambitious new development plan (1975–80), costing over £2000 million, is being substantially financed from its oil revenues. Dearer oil, however, can only have disastrous effects on those poor countries without oil. The twenty-five poorest countries are falling further behind, having few commodities they can export to set against extra oil costs, and it was symptomatic that the

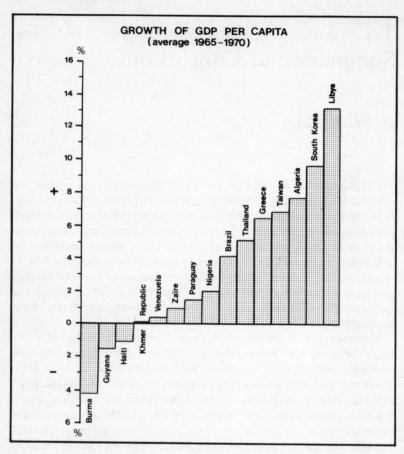

Figure 20   Growth of GDP *per capita* for selected countries, 1965–70

first objections to the 1975 rise in oil prices came from one of the poorest countries in the Third World – Tanzania.

Two potentially hopeful lines of thought about Third World development counterbalance the rather gloomy predictions which characterise contemporary discussion. In the first place there is now widespread acceptance of the fact that most less-developed countries cannot improve their lot without aid of some kind from developed countries. So far help has not been remarkable in amount or in the terms upon which aid has been offered. The aid is not yet as large as that recommended by UN agencies, but there are signs that it is being used more effectively. Channelling aid into growth points within a country or concentrating aid into areas of poverty and distress may express opposite views about how to apply aid most effectively; but both are preferable to the practice of scattering the benefits of aid too thinly over too wide a range of problems and areas.

Second, there seems to be an increasing acceptance of the view that poor countries have legitimate aspirations with regard to a fuller entry into the existing channels of world trade. Until recently attempts to change the pattern of world trade between the 'North' and 'South' have met with limited sympathy from the developed 'North'. One reason for this changing attitude is doubtless the recognition that by AD 2000 the Third World will contain more than three-quarters of the world's population. The huge size of the Third World's population, taken together with its high rate of increase, presents tremendous opportunities for the developed world. Such an enormous and growing market cannot be ignored by the industrial developed nations.

On the other hand, the continuing population explosion is seen by some observers as constituting a serious problem, and it is in some quarters suggested that the control of population growth is a most important first step in trying to raise living standards in Third World countries. Such a viewpoint, however, is now being seriously questioned. Certainly there is no simple correlation between low rates of population growth and high rates of economic growth. Countries with high population growth rates are among the most prosperous of the less-developed countries. In Iran, *per capita* income rose from $400 in 1969 to more than $1400 in 1975, despite a rise in population of more than 7 million; this represents a rate of increase of about 14 per cent per annum. The population explosion does, of course, constitute a problem, but present rapid rates of population growth need not necessarily inhibit economic progress and they may offer opportunities.

A long-needed adjustment in the terms of trade of the primary producing countries of the Third World is beginning to take place, though not all the less-developed countries are likely to benefit equally. In the recent commodity boom, India and other countries which import food grains, metals or fuels suffered, whereas Latin American, West African and south-east Asian countries which export minerals, timber, rubber and edible oils gained somewhat.

Commodity Booms and Slumps

Nevertheless, any commodity boom, when viewed overall, should be substantially beneficial to Third World countries. Whereas the value of international aid has been running recently at about $40000 million a year in less-developed countries, their own increase in foreign earnings exceeded this figure by a wide margin in many cases. And if Third World countries organise themselves together into commodity groups, they are likely to be in a position to press successfully for higher prices. The effect that all this will have on relations between the developed and less-developed countries are potentially enormous and salutary. On the other hand, slumps, or a world recession, must hit hardest the world's poorest countries.

Assumptions and criteria for judgement of and action about Third World development are complex. Is it true that 'development' must necessarily imply a rapid and cumulative increase in per capita incomes? Do all Third World countries really wish to follow the same path – or any path – towards material progress as that followed by Western nations? Does the Chinese model of development have greater relevance to the problems and aspirations of Third World countries than Western models of development?

Even in material terms the effectiveness and relevance of the Chinese experience seem undeniable. In 1971 China registered one of the highest growth rates in the world for the combined production of agriculture and industry, 10 per cent. This figure was exceeded only by Romania, Brazil and Iran, equalled by that of South Korea, and it compared favourably with rates of 6.1 per cent for Japan, 6 per cent for the USSR, and 2.7 per cent for the United States. Perhaps of greater importance is the question: does the Chinese model not place a proper emphasis on equity and social justice? Can one not find in most Third World countries those qualities of life which some Western countries are in serious danger of losing? And do not the ecological implications of rapid economic growth in developed countries challenge the practicability and desirability of our conventional, materialistic and narrowly conceived notions of development?

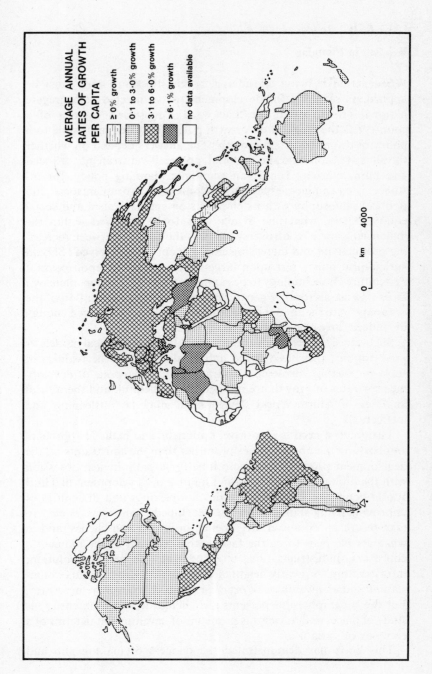

AVERAGE ANNUAL
RATES OF GROWTH
PER CAPITA

≥ 0% growth
0·1 to 3·0% growth
3·1 to 6·0% growth
>6·1% growth
no data available

0   4000
        km

Figure 21   Global rates of growth *per capita*, 1970–2

Realism in Planning

When action is being considered, a realistic framework must be applied. Is planning for development to be directed at aggregate national growth or at the 'backward', 'depressed' regions of a country? Is the creation of 'growth poles' felt to be preferable to a policy of dispersed urban growth? The answers depend on whether the aims are economic and material, political and strategic, or social and humanitarian. Tanzanian economic planning policy, for instance, is meaningless except in the context of Tanzanian social and political philosophy with its emphasis on egalitarianism and social equity. Again, what line of action is to be followed within the 'balanced growth' controversy? How is the conflict between increasing productivity and increasing employment to be resolved? Should agricultural policy rest upon large-scale schemes or upon peasant agriculture? Is technology to be capital-intensive or labour-intensive? Does one use sectoral or general priorities in the organisation of the economy? Are the spatial implications of development given enough or, indeed, any place in planning policies?

Such decisions need more than a checklist of theoretical models or prescriptions; they need to be judged also against the realities of socio-political or ideological aspirations. Comparisons of development or rates of growth are not necessarily helpful, and theoretical analyses of Third World development may be misleading and ineffectual.

The greatest need is a positive, optimistic and realistic approach, emphasising the opportunities of, rather than the constraints in, the development process. This is no time for a pathological obsession with the limitations, obstacles and failures of development in Third World countries. Overcome by the complexities and difficulties of improving living standards in less-developed countries, it is easy to take refuge in 'doomster' arguments, in jargon and clichés, and in whatever happens to be the fashionable panacea of the moment – education, industrialisation, birth control, the green revolution, infrastructure. A greatly heightened sense of environmental circumstances and an awareness of every problem of change are necessary. For the geographer this presents a challenge: he has to intensify his study of places and to view his problems of development in terms of a complex of variables.

This book has demonstrated the dangers of making glib and

superficial generalisations about less-developed countries, of making them seem as if they constitute a homogeneous group with distinctive characteristics and problems. Several chapters have emphasised the need to respect the enormous variety and complexity of the Third World and to undertake development with due attention to the inherent qualities and limitations of each specific environment, to the cultural appropriateness of proposed change, and to the distinctive personality and 'mix' of problems in any particular country. There is certainly some danger of underplaying the uniqueness of a less-developed country's problems since, as one contributor has written, the whole question of technological transfer 'involves specific people in specific places'. While it is legitimate and necessary for the geographer to continue his search for common denominators, key factors and regularities in the development process, his statements and views must match up to the realities of specific problems in particular areas. Increasingly, there seems to be a clear recognition of the fact that there need be no conflict between the 'theoretical' and 'unique' approaches; the divergence in viewpoints between geographers is lessening as both sides adopt less extreme positions.

These pages also raise the issue of the level and quality of perception revealed by those who are genuinely concerned to say and do something about Third World development. Within developed countries, the overriding need is not for more sophisticated theoretical analyses but for appreciation and greater understanding of development as seen through the eyes of those who are trying to improve their own societies and economies in their own very specific ways. It is, of course, exceedingly difficult for a Western observer to be sure he is on exactly the right wavelength. It is difficult for him to avoid being condescending or patronising. And unless he keeps his own assumptions and criteria for judgement under review, it will be impossible to avoid being irrelevant.

For this reason, and to encourage a much higher level of realistic thinking and writing about Third World development, there is an urgent need for more geographers and other scholars in Third World countries to write about their own problems, opportunities and philosophies of development. Certainly, within the Third World countries there is clear recognition of the difficulties with which they are faced in their efforts to achieve development and it is here exactly that one finds the most positive, realistic and dynamic thinking about development.

It is recognised that the future prosperity of newly independent territories still depends greatly upon what happens in the rest of the world. A deepening of the world depression would halt and drastically reverse the commodity boom on which the hopes of so many Third World countries have been pinned. Continued failure to make any real progress in UNCTAD will frustrate the trading potential of poorer countries. The way in which primary producing countries are still extremely susceptible to fluctuations in world demand and prices for their commodities has been recently well demonstrated by the changes in copper and cocoa prices, and any refusal on the part of oil-producing countries to provide some kind of two-tier pricing system to give oil to the poorest nations on preferential terms can so easily cancel out the benefits of aid and development. It may be that indexing oil prices will prove to be the most practicable solution to this kind of problem, but in any case these are issues over which the poorer Third World countries can have little or no control.

Perhaps it is only by a radical change in development aims, by a ruthless re-examination of assumptions about the social and political contexts of development, by self-help and by encouraging national economic independence as far as possible that Third World countries can have any future at all. Is it desirable that Third World countries should adopt Chinese, Tanzanian or similar models rather than those of the capitalist Western world? Each country must make its own decision about such questions. Given the political will, firm legitimate government, an adequate administrative framework and a proper ideological commitment, each Third World country must strive to deal effectively with its own development problems and to realise its own particular aims of social, economic and political endeavour.

Further Reading

1   The Third World in Perspective (Mountjoy)

Clifford, J. and Osmond, G., *World Development Handbook*, London (1971)
Furtado, C., *Development and Underdevelopment*, Berkeley and Los Angeles (1974)
Hodder, B. W., *Economic Development in the Tropics*, London (1973)
Hutchinson, Sir J., *The Challenge of the Third World*, London (1975)
Mountjoy, A. B. (ed), *Developing the Underdeveloped Countries*, London (1971)
Spiegelglas, S. and Welsh, C. J., *Economic Development: Challenge and Promise*, New Jersey (1970)
Stamp, L. D., *Our Developing World*, London (1960)

2   Environmental Hazards (Eden)

Dasmann, R. F., Milton, J. P. and Freeman, P. H., *Ecological Principles for Economic Development*, London (1973)
Eden, M. J., Ecology and land development: the case of the Amazonian rainforest *Trans. Inst. Br. Geogr.*, **2**, (1978)
Ehrlich, P. R., Holdran, A. H. and Holdran, J. P., *Human Ecology: Problems and Solutions*, San Francisco (1973)
Gourou, P., *The Tropical World*, London (1973)
Hodder, B. W., *Economic Development in the Tropics*, London (1973)
Johnson, B. L. C., Recent developments in rice breeding and some implications for tropical Asia. *Geography*, **57** (1972) 307–20
Tosi, J. A. and Voertman, R. F., Some environmental factors in the economic development of the Tropics. *Econ. Geogr.*, **40** (1964) 189–205
Watters, R. F., *Shifting Cultivation in Latin America*, FAO, Rome (1971)

3   Fertile People in Infertile Lands (Clarke)

Borrie, W. D., *The Growth and Control of World Population*, London (1970)

Borrie, W. D., *Population, Environment and Society*, Auckland (1973)

Cipolla, C. M., *The Economic History of World Population*, 6th edn, Harmondsworth (1974)

Clarke, J. I., *Population Geography and the Developing Countries*, Oxford (1971)

Enke, S., The economic aspects of slowing population growth. *Econ. J.* (1966)

Parry, H. B., (ed) *Population and its Problems: A Plain Man's Guide*, London (1974)

Trewartha, G. T., *The Less Developed Realm: A Geography of its Population*, New York (1972)

United Nations, *The Determinants and Consequences of Population Trends*, Vol. 1 (1973)

Zelinsky, W., Kosinski, L. A. and Prothero, R. M., (eds) *Geography and a Crowding World: A symposium on population pressures upon physical and social resources in the developing lands*, London (1970)

4 Economic Planning (Patman)

Coates, B. E., Johnston, R. J. and Knox, P. L., *Geography and Inequality*, Oxford (1977)

Hagen, E. E., *On the Theory of Social Change*, Homewood, Ill. (1962)

Hirschman, A. O., *The Strategy of Economic Development*, Yale (1958)   (especially chapter 3)

Kunkel, J. H. Values and behaviour in economic development. *Econ. Dev. Cult. Change*, **XIII** no.3 (1964)

Lewis, A., *The Development Process*, UN, New York (1970)

Myrdal, G., *Economic Theory and Underdeveloped Regions*, London (1957)

Rostow, W. W., *The Stages of Economic Growth*, 2nd edn, Cambridge (1971)

Todaro, M. P., *Economic Development in the Third World* London, (1977)

United Nations Economic and Social Council report, *Problems and Practices of African Countries in the Compilation of Input-Output Tables*, New York (1971)

5 The Rural Revolution (Grigg)

Brown, L. R., and Finsterbusch, G. W., *Man and his Environment: Food*, London (1972)

Chakravarti, A., Green revolutions in India. *Ann. Ass. Am. Geogr*, **63,** (1973) 217–25

Chakravarti, A., Foodgrain sufficiency patterns in India. *Geogr. Rev.*, **60**, (1970) 208–28

Grigg, D., *The Harsh Lands: A study in agricultural development*, London (1970)

Jacoby, E. H., *Man and Land: the fundamental issue in development*, London (1971)

Ruthenberg, H., *Farming Systems in the Tropics*, London (1971)

Wharton, C. R., Jr (Ed.) *Subsistence agriculture and economic development*, Chicago (1969)

6 Reform of Agrarian Structures (Sutton)

Dorner, P., *Land Reform and Economic Development*, Harmondsworth (1972)

Dorner, P. and Kanel, D., The economic case for land reform: employment, income distribution and productivity. *Land Reform, Land Settlement and Co-operatives*, 1971 (I) 1–16

El Ghonemy, M. R., Land reform and economic development in the Near East. *Land Econ.*, **44** (1968) 36–49

Jacoby, E. H., *Man and Land: The Fundamental Issues in Development*, London (1971)

Jeffries, A., Agrarian reform in Chile. *Geography*, **3** (1971) 221–30

King, R., *Land Reform: The Italian Experience*, London (1973)

King, R., *Land Reform. A World Survey*, London (1977)

Koo, A. Y. C., *The Role of Land Reform in Economic Development: A Case Study of Taiwan*, New York (1968)

Sutton, K., Agrarian Reform in Algeria: The Conversion of Projects into Action, *Afrika Spectrum*, Hamburg I (1974) 50–68.

Sutton, K., The Progress of Algeria's Agrarian Reform and its Settlement Implications, *The Maghreb Review*, **2** (1977) 5–6

Warriner, D., *Land Reform in Principle and Practice*, Oxford (1969)

The FAO in Rome publishes twice yearly a useful journal – *Land Reform, Land Settlement and Co-operatives* – which contains articles, documents and bibliographies on agrarian reform.

7 Technology and the Third World (Bowen-Jones)

Dumont, R., *False Start in Africa*, London (1969)

Intermediate Technology Publications, *Appropriate Technology* (a quarterly journal)

McRobie, G., Technology for development – 'Small is Beautiful'. *J. R. Soc. Arts.*, **CXII** (1974) 214–24

Myrdal, G., The transfer of technology to underdeveloped countries. *Scient. Am.*, **231** (1974) 172–82
Schumacher, E.F., *Small is Beautiful*, London (1973)

8   The Infrastructure Gap (Hilling)

Fromm, G. (ed), *Transport Investment and Economic Development*, Washington DC (1965)
Hirschman, A. O., *The Strategy of Economic Development*, Yale (1958)
Hoyle, B. S., (ed), *Transport and Development*, London (1973)
Hoyle, B. S. (ed), *Spatial Aspects of Development*, London (1974)
Hoyle, B. S. and Hilling, D. (eds), *Seaports and Developments in Tropical Africa*, London (1970)
McMaster, D. M. (ed), *Transport in Africa*, African Studies Centre, Edinburgh (1970)
Myrdal, G., *The Challenge of World Poverty*, Harmondsworth (1970)
Owen, W., *Strategy for Mobility*, London (1964)

9   Industrialisation in the Third World (Dickenson)

Davey, J., Industrial development in Rajasthan and Madhya Pradesh, India. *Trans. Inst. Br. Geog.*, **49** (1970) 183–200
Dickenson, J., Industrial estates in Brazil. *Geography*, **55** (1970) 326–29
Dickenson, J., Imbalances in Brazil's industrialization. In B. S. Hoyle (ed) *Spatial Aspects of Development*, London (1974) pp. 291–306
Fairbairn, I., A survey of local industries in Western Samoa. *Pacif. Viewpoint*, **12** (1971) 103–22.
Freeberne, M., China promotes local industries. *Geogr. Mag.* **43** (1971) 505–11.
Gilbert, A., Industrial location theory: its relevance to an industrializing nation. In B. S. Hoyle (ed) *Spatial Aspects of Development*, London (1974) pp. 271–89
Gilbert, A., The process of industrial change. In *Latin American Development: a geographical perspective*, Harmondsworth (1974) pp. 39–82
Hay, A., Imports versus local production: a case study from the Nigerian cement industry. *Econ. Geogr.*, **47** (1971) 384–88.
Mabogunje, A., Manufacturing and the geography of development in tropical Africa. *Econ. Geogr.*, **49** (1973) 1–20
Mountjoy, A., *Industrialization and Developing Countries*, London (1978)
Okezie C. and Onyemelukwe, J., Industrial location in Nigeria. In F.E.I.

Hamilton (ed) *Spatial Perspectives on Industrial Organization and Decision Making*, London (1974) pp. 461–84

Robinson, R. (ed), *Industrialization in Developing Countries* Cambridge University Overseas Studies Committee, Cambridge (1965)

Sears, D., The role of industry in development: some fallacies, *J. Mod. Afr. Stud.*, **1** (1963) 461–5

Swindell, K., Industrialization in Guinea. *Geography*, **54** (1969) 456–8

Sutcliffe, R., *Industrial and underdevelopment*, London (1971)

10 Urbanisation in the Third World (Mountjoy)

Breese, G., *Urbanization in Newly Developing Countries*, London (1966)

Davis, K., *World Ubranization 1950–70*, 2 vols, Berkeley, California (1969, 1972)

Dwyer, D. J. (ed), *The City in the Third World*, London (1974)

Dwyer, D. J., *People and Housing in Third World Cities*, London (1975)

Friedmann, J. and Wulf, R., *The Urban Transition*, London (1975)

Hauser, P. M., *Urbanization in Latin America*, New York (1961)

McGee, T. G., *The South-East Asian City*, London (1967)

Mangin, W., Squatter settlements. *Scient. Am.*, **217** (1967) 21–9

Mangin, W., *Peasants in Cities*, Boston (1970)

Mountjoy, A. B., Urbanization, the squatter and development in the Third World. *Tijd. Ec. Soc. Geog.*, **67** (1976) 130–7

11 Rural Development and Rural Change (Siddle)

Brookfield, H., *Interdependent Development*, London (1975)

Chambers,R., *Settlement Schemes in Tropical Africa: a study of organization and development*, London (1969)

Dumont, R., *False Start in Africa*, London (1969)

Frank, A. G., *Capitalism and Underdevelopment in Latin America*, New York (1969)

Harvey, D., *Social Justice and the City*, chapter 6, London (1973)

Lipton, M., *Why Poor People Stay Poor: a study of urban bias in world development*, London (1977)

Sahlims, M., *Stone Age Economics*, London (1974)

Wilkinson, R. G., *Poverty and Progress*, London (1973)

Williams, R., *The Country and the City*, London (1973)

12 Aid for Needy Nations (Morgan)

Bhagwati, J., and Eckaus, R. S. (eds), *Foreign Aid*, Harmondsworth (1970)
Clifford, J. M., and Osmond, G., *World Development Handbook*, London (1971)
Hayter, Teresa, *Aid as Imperialism*, Harmondsworth 1971
OECD, Development Assistance Committee: Annual Report, (HMSO) London
Pearson, Lester B., *Partners in Development*, New York and London (1970)
Ward, B., and Bauer, P. T., *Two Views on Aid to Developing Countries*, Occasional paper no. 9, Institute of Economic Affairs, London (1966)
Mende, T., *From Aid to Recolonization*, London (1973)

13 Trade Growth for Development (Hilling)

Bhagwati, J. (ed), *International Trade*, Harmondsworth (1969)
Maizels, A., *Growth and Trade*, London (1970)
Maizels, A. (*et al*), *Exports and Growth in Developing Countries*, London (1968)
Myrdal, G., *The Challenge of World Poverty*, Harmondsworth (1970)
Pearson, L., *Partners in Development*, New York and London (1970)
Seers, D., *Development in a Divided World*, Harmondsworth (1970)
Streeten, P., *Trade Strategies for Development*, London (1973)
Thirlwall, A. P., When is trade more valuable than aid? *J. Dev. Stud.*, **13** (1), 1976, 35–41

14 Summary and Conclusions (Hodder)

Bairoch, Paul., *The Economic Development of the Third World Since 1900*, London (1975)
Brookfield, H., *Interdependent Development*, London (1975)
Furtado, C., *Development and Underdevelopment*, Berkeley and Los Angeles (1964)
Hodder, B. W., *Economic Development in the Tropics*, London (1973)
Hoyle, B. S., *Spatial Aspects of Development*, London (1974)

Notes on Contributors

Howard Bowen–Jones is Professor of Geography and Director of the Centre of Middle Eastern and Islamic Studies, University of Durham

John I. Clarke is Professor of Geography, University of Durham

John P. Dickenson is Lecturer in Geography, University of Liverpool

Michael J. Eden is Lecturer in Geography, Bedford College, University of London

David Grigg is Reader in Geography, University of Sheffield

David Hilling is Senior Lecturer in Geography, Bedford College, University of London

B. W. Hodder is Professor of Geography, School of Oriental and African Studies, University of London

W. T. W. Morgan is Professor of Geography, University of Jos, Nigeria

Alan B. Mountjoy is Reader in Geography, Bedford College, University of London

Colin R. Patman is Lecturer in Geography, Bedford College, University of London

David J. Siddle is Senior Lecturer in Geography, University of Liverpool

Keith Sutton is Lecturer in Geography, University of Manchester

Index